Robert Tavernor
studied architecture in London
and at the British School in Rome, then received a PhD in
architectural history from the University of Cambridge. He
has maintained his interest in both fields: he is an architect in
private practice, and Lecturer in the School of Architecture
and Building Engineering at the University of Bath. He has
been a visiting lecturer and critic at leading schools of
architecture in Britain and the United States, and, with
Joseph Rykwert and Neil Leach, he translated and edited
Alberti's *On the Art of Building in Ten Books* (1988).

WORLD OF ART

This famous series
provides the widest available
range of illustrated books on art in all its aspects.
If you would like to receive a complete list
of titles in print please write to:
THAMES AND HUDSON
30 Bloomsbury Street, London WC1B 3QP
In the United States please write to:
THAMES AND HUDSON INC.
500 Fifth Avenue, New York, New York 10110

ROBERT TAVERNOR

PALLADIO AND PALLADIANISM

With 163 illustrations

THAMES AND HUDSON

To Denise

© 1991 Thames and Hudson Ltd, London

First published in the United States in 1991 by
Thames and Hudson Inc., 500 Fifth Avenue,
New York, New York 10110

Library of Congress Catalog Card Number 90-70179

Printed and bound in Singapore

Contents

The scholarship in this subject area is awesome, and my debts are many. For their writings I am especially grateful to James Ackerman, Lionello Puppi and Howard Burns on Palladio; John Summerson, John Harris and Roy Strong on Inigo Jones; Rudolf Wittkower, John Harris and Joseph Rykwert on the English Palladians; and Fiske Kimball, Frederick Nichols, and Dumas Malone on Thomas Jefferson. I am grateful too for the comments raised by Professor Ackerman after he read a draft of the text on Palladianism in America, and I was also fortunate to be able to meet and receive an early response to my outline for the book from Douglas Lewis of the National Gallery, Washington, and from Mario Valmarana and Charles Brownell of the University of Virginia. Professor Brownell made available to me the research papers of his M. Phil. students, and I was given access to the excellent archives on Jefferson in the Architecture Faculty Library at Charlottesville. In the United Kingdom, I am particularly indebted to Deborah Howard of Edinburgh University, who generously shared with me her own recent researches and later read a first draft of the typescript, and also helped with elusive photographs. Ian Campbell of Cambridge University, and Richard Schofield of Nottingham University, provided me with the sort of frank criticism on the text that only long-term friends have the courage to give. Emily Lane provided invaluable criticism which was based on her substantial knowledge of the material. Finally, my thanks go to Anne Engel for her initial act of faith, and to Joseph Rykwert, my own 'master and guide'.

R. T.

Andrea Palladio is probably the most famous architect of the Western world. His work has enjoyed several revivals since his death in 1580, and his buildings and writings have influenced the course of architecture to the present day. His popularity today is founded on the accessibility of his surviving buildings in northern Italy, and the excellent settings and condition in which many of them exist. There is sheer joy to be found in 'discovering' a palace by him in the narrow streets of Vicenza; in appreciating the dignity that his Basilica lends to that city's main civic space; in coming upon one of his villas in its country setting; and in emerging from the tight winding streets of Venice into the Piazza and Piazzetta S. Marco and seeing, across the blue waters of the Lagoon, the white stones of his church of S. Giorgio.

Palladio was undoubtedly more fortunate than many other great artists and architects in that he had the opportunity to build many of his designs for villas, palaces, churches and public buildings in his own lifetime, a success in its own right for which he deserves to be celebrated. But more than the quantity of buildings, their quality has led them to become prime examples of a particular approach to architecture, of design *all'antica* (in the antique manner), in which he excelled.

His course in this direction was set when his talents as a stonemason were recognized and developed by certain noblemen living in the Venetian Republic, in the vicinity of Vicenza. The training and experience he gained from them allowed him to develop, over many years, his own interpretation of the classical style that had recently spread to northern Italy from its source in Florence and Rome. For he had made thorough studies of Roman architecture, and he was familiar with ancient and Renaissance theory and practice, a fertile base to which he brought a new vitality. His designs, while pursuing the rigours of the classical language – of propriety, order, and proportion – are infused with an infectious humanity, a love of virtue and good action, which shines through his buildings even today: their scale,

8

form, details and materials harmonize with the rural landscape and contribute to the quality of civic life in a way that has proved to be inspirational for the followers of the theories he espoused.

His followers have been numerous, and almost as famous. They followed because they shared his commitment to the same classical, natural principles: a philosophy of life as well as of design. The Roman architect Marcus Vitruvius Pollio provided a text in the 1st century BC which was their main introduction to ancient theory, yet they were called 'Palladians' because Palladio was their acknowledged basis for a modern interpretation of classical values.

Palladians of the first rank visited the remains of Roman antiquity, and Palladio's buildings, in order to test theory against practice, an invaluable procedure that was not open to every aspiring classical architect. Back at home, the drawings of Palladio, especially those in his *Quattro libri dell'architettura* (Four Books on Architecture) which he had published towards the end of his career, in 1570, were the most valuable record of his 'modern' classicism and the basis of the Palladian movement. As enthusiasm for his architecture spread, translations of his texts and engravings of his designs were made more widely available. Through the popularization of his work the purity of his message was corrupted, and the ambitions for society through architecture of the true Vitruvio-Palladians were undermined, though not without some spectacular architectural successes.

This book – an introduction to a vast and complex subject – sets out to highlight some of the successes of Palladio, as well as those of his followers in the English-speaking world, by exploring their various interpretations of the architectural theory that motivated and united them. Inigo Jones, the first of the great English Palladians, in the early 17th century; Lord Burlington a little over a hundred years later; and the last of the Anglo-Palladians in America, Thomas Jefferson, around 1800, will be singled out to trace individual readings of the Vitruvian message after Palladio. These men of action revolutionized the practice of architecture in their own times with the enhancing of society a primary objective. This issue remains pertinent today as the role of the 'active citizen' is under scrutiny once again.

ANDREA
PALLADIO
ARCHITETO
VICENTINO.
1576.

1   Portrait of Andrea Palladio in his late sixties, by his friend Giambattista Maganza.

PART ONE

The foundations of Palladio's architecture

I THE VITRUVIAN RENAISSANCE IN ITALY

Rummaging through one of the great literary treasure troves of Europe in search of Latin manuscripts, the celebrated Florentine humanist and Latinist Poggio Bracciolini discovered in the monastic library of St Gallen in Switzerland a copy of *De architectura* by Vitruvius superior to any then known. This find was of paramount importance to the reawakened interest in classical art and architecture in early 15th-century Florence. For although the manuscript was notoriously obscure, and unillustrated, its text remained the only key to a true understanding of the ruins of Roman antiquity which were still to be marvelled at throughout Italy.

From early scholastic interpretations of Vitruvius, and investigations of classical buildings themselves, the Italian Renaissance of the arts and architecture burgeoned with the talent and application of individuals into distinctive branches of expression of the *all'antica* style. Many names are known to us still from this period, but in architecture perhaps none is as familiar as that of Andrea Palladio. Not only has his work survived his own lifetime to be appreciated by subsequent generations, but, quite uniquely, he inspired a movement, Palladianism, which supported his particular search for classical beauty in architecture.

Andrea Palladio was a product of Italian humanism, which is characterized by a revived intellectual concern for the writings and physical remains of classical antiquity. It established itself first in Quattrocento Florence, where the 'rebirth' of art and architecture was its most tangible manifestation. The ferment of ideas there led to discoveries of the theory and practice of the ancients. Painters rediscovered and reformulated the laws of perspective, sculptors 'ideal' human proportions. Architects, beginning with Filippo Brunelleschi, reputedly made first-hand studies of the surviving remains of antique architecture, especially in Rome.

Vitruvius had advocated the study and imitation of Nature as one of the most important pursuits for an architect. For Nature leads to Beauty, which is fundamental to the practice of architecture, once

Utility and Strength have been achieved in a building. These three criteria, of *utilitas*, *firmitas* and *venustas*, were to be pursued by the application of rigorous laws learnt from Nature: every aspect of an architectural endeavour was to be controlled by rational principles.

Acknowledgment of these principles meant too that buildings having different uses should conform to specific configurations, according to what Vitruvius called *decorum*. Vitruvius determined the precise delineations of model buildings: the Greek and Roman theatre, the temple and the basilica were among the prime exemplars of public buildings. *Decorum* extends to the characterization of a particular building through ornament, of which Vitruvius defined three principal types identified by the proportions and details of their columns, entablatures and associated mouldings.

These 'orders', as they are called, are arranged hierarchically. The least refined and prestigious is the Doric, which has a column with the shortest shaft and plainest capital (an Italian variation of this Greek order, the Tuscan, is plainer still). Then comes the Ionic with its more slender column and a capital which has curled elements called 'volutes'; and then the Corinthian, which Vitruvius considered the most elegant of the three, with the slenderest shaft and a capital distinguished by two ranks of acanthus leaves and fern-like stems at the corners. With each of the classical orders comes a series of specific details which give it a discernible character. The Corinthian is the most ornate of the Vitruvian canon, but the 15th-century theorist and architect Leon Battista Alberti (1404–72) included a fourth antique type, the 'Italic' order, which came to be known as the Composite, the most splendid of them all: this has a capital composed of volutes and acanthus leaves, combining features of the Ionic with the Corinthian. Much energy was directed to interpreting the theory of classical ornament in the Quattrocento, and to establishing a coherent body of architecture that would equal the achievements of antiquity.

Early successes in designing and building according to Vitruvian rules were augmented by the first treatise on architecture since antiquity, *De re aedificatoria* (On the Art of Building), by Alberti. This was begun as a commentary on Vitruvius but grew into an original treatise on architecture which paid homage to Vitruvian values, and elucidated some of Vitruvius's obscurer passages. Arranged in ten books, each dealing with distinct subjects relating to why and how architecture is made, it took the Renaissance beyond Florence to the other intellectual centres of Italy.

Florence, so long the centre of excellence in Italy, was being rivalled by the growing power and authority of Rome towards the end of the 15th century. Rome had been under the influence of several humanist popes since the election in 1446 of Nicholas V, who had embarked on the rebuilding of the city in order to restore something of its antique glory. With the advice of Alberti, who presented him with a manuscript version of his architectural treatise in the early 1450s, and the Florentine architect Bernardo Rossellino, Nicholas restored part of the city walls and aqueducts, and commenced an ambitious programme of works at the Vatican and the ancient Capitol. Pius II continued where Nicholas left off, and by the end of the century Julius II, who was no less ambitious than his predecessors, was planning a vast new church of St Peter, exploiting the brilliance of his architect, Donato Bramante, who with a circle of talented artists and architects went on to transform the Vatican and the city. Rome by the early 16th century was once again a great political and spiritual centre and was regarded as the earthly successor of Jerusalem, since Jerusalem was then in the hands of the 'pagan' Turks.

Rome attracted the finest artists and architects. They went there to study the antique remains, and to seek work in the Vatican or from the immensely rich noble families resident in the city. Many of them came from Florence, which remained influential. The rest of Italy was on the edge of this classical Renaissance, and responded gradually to the supremacy of Roman and Florentine culture.

In northern Italy local building tradition continued to predominate with only superficial stylistic acknowledgments to the revival of antiquity. This was true of the state of Milan, as well as of Venice and its dependent cities which included Padua, Verona and the much smaller Vicenza. Venice, whose empire had contracted as the Ottoman empire expanded, was crippled by the wars of the League of Cambrai, when Rome joined forces with the Holy Roman Emperor and the Kings of France and Aragon under Julius II in 1509 to seize Venetian possessions. The struggle that ensued was not concluded finally until the Peace of Bologna twenty years later. The financial burden of this period effectively curbed new building.

In Venice, the new classicism of Florence and Rome was blended with indigenous preferences for Gothic and for the more exotic Byzantine forms of her empire. Mauro Codussi (c. 1440–1504) stands out for his *all'antica* approach; but it is doubtful whether he ever went to Rome: the Roman ruins of Verona and Rimini were probably his sole experiences of antiquity, and the Tempio Malatestiano in Rimini by Alberti his only direct confrontation with the modern classicism then emerging. The rigorous Vitruvian approach to architecture, the so-called High Renaissance, of which Bramante was the focus, was slow in coming. Its eventual arrival was precipitated by a catastrophe in Rome.

Early in 1527, Rome was invaded by troops of the Emperor Charles V who was responding to the anti-Imperial league which Pope Clement VII had joined. His forces were composed largely of Lutheran mercenaries intent on revenge for the persecution they had suffered by order of the Catholic Church. The pope wisely sought refuge in the Castel S. Angelo during the early stages of an occupation that lasted until February of the following year, and although he was left unscathed, the Sack left the social structure of the city in tatters. There was no immediate future in Rome for those intent on fame and fortune, and artists and intellectuals dispersed, mainly northwards to the major city states and Venetian dominions of the Po valley. The most important refugee for the architectural future of Venice was the Florentine sculptor and architect Jacopo Sansovino (1486–1570).

Sansovino had practised successfully in Florence and Rome for most of his early life. He drifted northwards after 1521, following the disappointment of having his design for the church of S. Giovanni dei Fiorentini in Rome assigned by Pope Leo X to another architect for construction. He was drawn to Venice where he found work advising on the restoration of the domes of St Mark's, but returned to Rome believing that the newly elected pope Clement VII was about to resurrect his project, which had been abandoned on Leo X's death. This hope was dashed in 1527, and he returned to Venice, where he stayed for the remaining forty-three years of his life. Initially, he was supported there by Doge Andrea Gritti, who involved him in further restoration work on the ducal basilica of St Mark's. Recognition led to his appointment as *Proto*, or superintendent, of the Procuracy of St Mark's, a much envied position which gave him direct responsibility for building works in the political centre of Venice.

Here Sansovino achieved his greatest architectural success. With his designs for the Zecca or Mint (1536), the Library of St Mark's (1537), and the Loggetta (1538) at the base of the much older Campanile, Sansovino brought a new magnificence to the Piazzetta S. Marco, which extends from the end of the Piazza S. Marco to the water. The
2 Library lent the edge of the Piazzetta a unity which balanced the

2   Sansovino: Library of St Mark's, Venice, 1537ff, viewed from across the Piazzetta S. Marco.

Doge's Palace opposite, and so allowed St Mark's to become the natural focus at the end of the space. In this way, Sansovino created a new urban forum at the landing-stage for official visitors to Venice. Although not completed in his lifetime, the building brought Sansovino great fame for its fusion of antique Roman ideals (such as the correct Vitruvian hierarchical and proportional use of the classical orders) with the Venetian fondness for rich ornament. The façade, in two tiers, consists of a major trabeated system with a subsidiary arcuated system threaded through it, Doric below and Ionic above. The major Ionic order stands on pedestals linked by balustrades, and both tiers are enriched by keystone heads and figures in the spandrels of the arches. The deep crowning entablature incorporates garlands and oval windows in the frieze; the roof is edged by a balustrade above which heroic statues and obelisks are silhouetted against the skyline. This is a highly embellished version of Roman classicism which is peculiarly Venetian: it was in marked contrast to the giant orders and surface simplicity of Michelangelo's Capitoline palaces in Rome started at much the same time.

More emphatically Roman was the theory and practice of two other refugees from the Sack of Rome, Sebastiano Serlio and Gian Giorgio Trissino. Serlio (1475–1554) was a Bolognese painter turned architect who had worked in the Vatican workshop under Bramante and Raphael. He acknowledged another famed painter-architect in the same circle, Baldassare Peruzzi, as his primary architectural mentor. Trissino, a nobleman and an intimate of Clement VII and Charles V, had known Serlio in Rome, and possibly met up with him in Bologna, where they both stayed immediately after the Sack. After Bologna, Trissino and Serlio settled in the Veneto, Trissino moving to Cricoli, just outside Vicenza, whilst Serlio went at first to Venice.

Trissino (1478–1550) was neither an artist nor an architect but a gifted diplomat and a brilliant Aristotelian scholar who had a profound concern for all things antique, from literature to architecture. His skills were primarily literary rather than visual. He had an ambition to create an academy in the Veneto along the lines of the academy in Florence of Lorenzo de' Medici, or its counterpart in

3   Serlio: garden elevation of Raphael's Villa Madama, from Book III, 1540/84.

4   Gian Giorgio Trissino: entrance front of the Villa Trissino at Cricoli, 1537–38. Note the subtle differences in the articulation of windows and niches compared to Serlio's illustration (opposite).

Rome of which Bembo and Castiglione were members before the Sack, and he determined to use his own villa at Cricoli to this end. It is possible that he consulted Serlio on the modernizations which he felt were necessary to create the proper humanistic setting for the Accademia Trissiniana, and building work was under way by 1537.

Both men had admired the villa on the slopes of Monte Mario, just outside Rome, that Raphael had designed for Cardinal Giulio de' Medici, known as the Villa Madama after a subsequent occupant. Serlio published his own version of the garden elevation of the Villa ⟨3⟩ Madama in Venice in 1540, in the third of his Seven Books on Architecture. (These were published together posthumously in 1584 and again in 1619 as *Tutte l'opere d'architettura et prospettiva*.) In 1537 Trissino adopted a very similar design for the façade at Cricoli, ⟨4⟩ presumably following Serlio's original drawing. It is thought likely that for the work Trissino would have used the finest stonemasons in Vicenza, the Pedemuro workshop, and that through this he became acquainted with one of their assistants, Andrea della Gondola, the future 'Palladio'.

Andrea was a native of Padua, where he had been born in 1508, the son of an artisan who prepared and installed millstones, Pietro della Gondola, and 'lame' Marta, on 30 November, the feast day of St Andrew. Through this combination of parentage and date he was known as Andrea di Pietro or Andrea della Gondola. The name 'Andrea Palladio', under which he achieved world-wide fame, came with his rebirth some thirty years later, at the Accademia Trissiniana at Cricoli. It was there that Andrea received an intellectual education only rarely offered to someone who had begun life so humbly. His new name, probably conferred on him by Trissino, marked the learning potential and ability which his humanist mentor presumably recognized. Indeed, it is likely that Trissino had a mission for Andrea. His earlier training as a stonemason coupled with his subsequent education enabled him to become a humanist architect – that is, a fully rounded individual who would be able to propel society towards humanist ideals through the act of building.

The name 'Palladio' appeared first of all in an epic poem that Trissino published as *L'Italia liberata dai Gotthi* (Italy freed from the Goths) in 1547. Trissino had begun writing this before he met Andrea, though it is not known when he cast the guardian angel Palladio into the plot. This 'Palladio' was a key figure who, through his support of the Emperor Justinian's troops, was instrumental in expelling the Goths from Italy. He guides his ward Belisarius, the commander of Justinian's forces, through an enemy-occupied palace, an act which saves Belisarius and his men from defeat. Moreover, he was an expert on the architecture of the palace, and takes time to describe its materials, measurements and proportions in considerable detail. The wisdom and vision of this angel prompted Trissino to find a suitable name: his choice may have been influenced by the comparable virtues of Pallas Athena, or he may have been alluding to the talisman in her image, known as the Palladium, which the Romans believed Aeneas had brought to Italy where it later safeguarded Rome. Andrea's adoption of an Italianized version of this name may have been inspired by the actions of Trissino's authoritative guide and interpreter of Vitruvian classicism, who would help to vanquish the Gothic. A less dramatic interpretation is that his name derives from that of a 4th-century Roman writer on agrarian culture, Palladius, for it was Andrea's response to the architecture of the farmhouse as villa that first established his independent reputation.

Andrea had arrived in Vicenza when in his mid-teens, accompanied by his father. He may have been introduced to the city by his god-father, Vincenzo de' Grandi, a local sculptor, who no doubt smoothed his way to being inscribed as an assistant in the Vicenza guild of ma-sons and stonecutters in April 1524. He had been apprenticed already to a Paduan stonemason, Bartolomeo Cavazza, but had served only eighteen months of a specified six-year apprenticeship before moving to Vicenza. Initially Cavazza had resisted this breach of articles, but later he relented in order that Andrea might continue his training with Giovanni da Porlezza of the Pedemuro workshop in Vicenza. Andrea's determination to break from Padua did not prevent him from remaining on friendly terms with his former employer, even when he went on to form a close working relationship with Giovanni da Porlezza. It is likely that his abilities were noticed by these men, and his talent appears to have been matched by his personal charm.

This was remarked on by Paolo Gualdo, who wrote a biography of Palladio in 1616, and it seems to have influenced his association with Trissino. Gualdo observed: 'he developed a very close relationship with the Vicentine humanist Gian Giorgio Trissino, one of the greatest scholars of his time. Finding Palladio to be a young man of

5   Portrait of Gian Giorgio Trissino by Vincenzo Catena, c. 1525.

very spirited character and with a great aptitude for science and mathematics, Trissino encouraged his natural abilities by training him in the precepts of Vitruvius.' This education began at Cricoli, a rural retreat ideal for study and reflection.

4   The *all'antica* villa that Trissino had created reflected his humanist aspirations, and was the outward manifestation of the curriculum the Academy offered for the benefit of young Vicentine nobles: Study, Arts and *Virtù*, notions celebrated in appropriate inscriptions over three of the villa's doorways. Music was the principal art. Other subjects included astronomy, geography and philosophy. Latin and Greek texts were used which, by example, encouraged an awareness of the well-rounded individual as a vital member of society – the true meaning of *virtù* advocated by all humanists. This concept was important for an aspiring architect. As Alberti had written in his architectural treatise, 'there is nothing to which a man should devote more care, more effort and attention than to *virtù*', because to produce excellent buildings which mirror the perfection of Nature the architect needed to be a moral and cultivated individual. Education was the key to this.

The extent of Andrea's involvement within the rigorous and demanding curriculum of the Accademia Trissiniana is not certain. It is doubtful whether he mastered Greek, but that he had a good working grasp of Latin is suggested by his subsequent architectural and literary career. Trissino himself had made a thorough study of Vitruvius and plainly was an architectural enthusiast. His own designs survive, including one for the layout of the ancient house described by Vitruvius. They are carefully contrived and proportioned, though their sketchy lines contain no sense of the materiality of a real building. This is where Andrea was able to contribute his experience, which Trissino committed himself to supplement using his knowledge of Vitruvius and the principles of natural philosophy.

There were no local architects in Vicenza, and when architectural expertise was required there, particularly for any major building work, outsiders were called in. This was the case with the rebuilding of the Palazzo della Ragione or Palace of Justice. The Palazzo (known since Palladio's later involvement as the 'Basilica'), built between 1449 and 1460, consisted of a large upper chamber set over ground floor shops separated by passageways. Later in the century it was wrapped by a two-storey colonnade, of which the western portion, towards the Cathedral, promptly collapsed. Over the next fifty years a succession of prominent architects were brought in from Venice to advise on its future, and in April 1538, the month when the villa at Cricoli was completed, Sansovino was paying his second visit to Vicenza with proposals for this prime civic building. He fared no better than any of his predecessors in obtaining the support of the Council, and within a year Serlio, a friend of Sansovino in Venice, had also been paid for some alternative proposals. (He was to be followed by Michele Sanmicheli from Verona in 1541 and by Giulio Romano from Mantua in 1542, as we shall see.)

Even if indecision reigned, the classical approach that these eminent architects had developed must have been making an impression on the Vicentine community. Through his association with Trissino, Andrea would have had opportunities to come into contact with their ideas and to obtain a direct understanding of the way in which the principles of classical architecture were then being interpreted. Trissino certainly seems to have been intent on exposing his pupil to influential people, ideas and environments over the new few years, and the two travelled together frequently.

Whilst Vicenza was to become his permanent base, Andrea moved back to Padua, where Trissino was also spending some time, for about two years between 1538 and 1540. He made two visits to Venice and one to Vicenza, where on 16 February 1539 he attended a theatrical performance staged by Serlio that was immensely impressive since it incorporated all the latest contrivances which Serlio had learnt in Rome. This event put the Vicentine nobles and their city on the cultural map, and boosted their own aspirations for Vicentine society, which was to be of direct benefit to Andrea. However, his immediate future was in Padua, where he was making the most of the introduction he had received into the circle of Alvise Cornaro, most likely through Trissino.

Alvise Cornaro (c. 1484–1566) was the author of the *Trattato della vita sobria* (Treatise on the Sober Life), which was celebrated in his lifetime, and an enthusiastic supporter of the literary and artistic community in Padua. His views complemented those of Trissino. Cornaro valued experience highly as 'the true foundation of the true sciences', and he might be expected to have been sympathetic to Andrea's background as a mason and the ambitions Trissino had for him as an architect. His humanism was realistic and pragmatic, as was his view of architecture, which not only ministers to 'the good comfort of man' but 'is beautiful as well'. This beauty was to be used for the enjoyment and benefit of everyone, to celebrate citizens and embellish cities, and not just for the 'edifices of emperors and princes'.

Nor was architecture to his mind the exclusive domain of the intellectual and scholar. It was correct to return to the study of first principles, but this research must be matched by first-hand experience of the physical remains of antiquity. Indeed, he wrote that he had learnt more 'from the ancient buildings than from the book of the divine Vitruvius'.

Trissino and Andrea were to heed this advice in a few years' time, but first there was still some groundwork to be done: in particular, Andrea needed to learn to express through drawings the ideas he was absorbing. Serlio was an important contact in this respect. He was an intimate of the Cornaro circle, and he had acknowledged his association with Cornaro in 1537 in the first of his publications to appear – Book IV, on the orders of architecture. The clarity of the illustrations there set a high graphic standard, and Andrea copied some of them directly.

Copying drawings is a very different experience from drawing buildings. It is likely that Cornaro, through his own collections and through his enlightened patronage of architecture, was able to offer Palladio some good practice in both areas. In the garden at the Casa
6   Cornaro he had built a single-storey stone loggia opening onto a court, which was a permanent setting for theatrical performances by and for his intellectual friends. The loggia, with its five arched openings, separated by Doric half-columns on pedestals, had been designed by the Veronese painter-architect Giovanni Maria Falconetto (1468–1535). The relationship between Cornaro and Falconetto was a very close one. They were companions who had explored the ruins of Rome together, and the loggia was the immediate outcome of their intellectual and artistic union. Built in 1524, it is the first rigorously all'antica building in the Veneto.

By the time of Andrea's introduction to the Cornaro circle Falconetto was dead, and another important garden pavilion was being erected to face onto the same court. This was built by
7,8 Falconetto's successor Andrea della Valle (d. 1577), after designs by Cornaro and perhaps Falconetto, and derived from classical models recorded in the drawings of Giuliano da Sangallo. Named the Odeo, it was intended for chamber music, and composed of a central octagonal room surrounded by smaller complementary spaces. Its rich interior decoration of frescoed landscape views and grotesques was an early indication for Andrea of the kind that had been made popular in Rome by Raphael, as well as the fusion of architecture and painting that Raphael's work exemplified. Serlio made drawings of

6   Falconetto: Loggia Cornaro,
Padua, 1524. (The top storey was
added later when the Odeo was
built.)

7, 8   Andrea della Valle, after
Alvise Cornaro and Falconetto(?):
Odeo Cornaro, Padua, *c.* 1530,
ground plan and octagonal central
chamber.

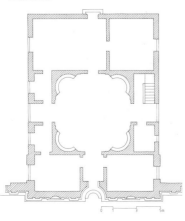

this building, along with variations on its centralized formality, which are illustrated in his books. In particular, it may be the nucleus from which the centralized plans of Palladio's later architecture developed.

If Cornaro was able to reinforce Trissino's architectural views with his own ideas and built examples, he was able also to put Andrea in contact with other powerful exponents of High Renaissance architecture. A distant cousin, Girolamo Cornaro, the Venetian commander in Padua, was at that time employing the fortification skills of Michele Sanmicheli (c. 1484–1559). Sanmicheli had trained in Rome with Bramante, and had formed a close friendship there with Antonio da Sangallo the Younger. Both architects had benefited from papal patronage and it was Clement VII who instructed them to inspect the papal fortifications together as the Imperial threat loomed large. Sanmicheli had the foresight to return home to Verona during the winter of 1526–27. There he set about strengthening the defences of the city, and designed some 'highly advanced, extremely original, and very beautiful' buildings, as Giorgio Vasari observed. His presence in Padua and the example of his palace architecture in Verona provided Andrea with a point of reference which is quite evident in his own later work.

The Cornaros proved to be of even more direct benefit to Palladio. Girolamo Cornaro had family connections with the Paduan branch of the Pisani family, and Alvise acted as administrator and architectural adviser to Cardinal Francesco Pisani, Bishop of Padua. Younger members of these families, Zorzon Cornaro (a son of Girolamo) and Vettor Pisani, became patrons, and Vettor's cousin Daniele Barbaro (who graduated from Padua University in 1540) and his brother Marc'Antonio became important collaborators as well as patrons.

It was normal for young nobles of the Venetian Republic who showed ability to complete their education at the famous university in Padua, as there was no university in Venice. By the mid-1550s a third of Vicenza's City Council were dottori, usually graduates from Padua. So it is not surprising that in the late 1530s many of Andrea's future patrons – Antonio Valmarana, Pietro Godi and Trissino's grandson Francesco – were either attending or had recently graduated from Padua University. At about the same time Andrea was beginning to establish his reputation as a designer independently of the Pedemuro workshop, and in 1540 he is referred to for the first time (as far as existing records show) as 'Andrea Palladio', and 'architect'.

PART TWO

Palladio's theory and practice of architecture

I IN PURSUIT OF NATURAL PRINCIPLES

In 1540, Palladio was back in Vicenza: he was aged thirty-two and had several major design projects in hand. The earliest of these, in 1537, was a continuation of building work, probably begun by the Pedemuro workshop, for the Villa Godi at Lonedo. In Vicenza, 9 Palladio designed his first palace, for the Civena family. The Palazzo Civena suggests the influence of his recent Paduan experience, as an early design blends proportions and details of the Loggia Cornaro with an illustration of a palace façade in Serlio's Book VII. As this was not published until 1575, it is assumed that Andrea had seen a preliminary drawing by Serlio. Another palace design bears direct 12 comparison both with Sanmicheli's Palazzo Pompei in Verona and 11 with Bramante's Palazzo Caprini in Rome (known more commonly as 'Raphael's House in the Borgo'), which Palladio had not yet seen but of which there were likely to have been drawings circulating amongst his contacts: one ended up in his own collection. 10

9 Palladio and the Pedemuro workshop: Villa Godi, Lonedo, after 1537.

10 *opposite* Bramante: Palazzo Caprini, Rome, sketched by an unknown 16th-century draughtsman.

11 *opposite below* Sanmicheli: Palazzo Pompei, Verona, *c.* 1530?

12 Palladio: an early design for a palace, with elements inspired by the architecture of Bramante and Sanmicheli.

At this stage, clearly, Palladio relied on secondary sources, emanating from the Rome exiles. In order to compete with them on equal terms he had to make his own direct studies of antiquity (as Cornaro had urged) and so discover the secrets of the ancients for himself. To this end he set off early in 1541 with Trissino, sponsored no doubt by the generosity of that nobleman, on a trip south which was to take in the major antiquities, particularly of Rome itself.

Although the trip was relatively brief (he was back in Vicenza by the autumn), this was the first of five visits to Rome which enabled him to study and draw many of the most famous monuments. He also obtained drawings which he copied, presumably to save time, and to which he sometimes added measurements that he had recorded from direct observations of the monument. Some Renaissance buildings were given similar attention: he saw and recorded works by Bramante (drawings of the Tempietto and of S. Biagio survive from this trip) and Raphael (Villa Madama), and he would undoubtedly have taken the opportunity to see the work of Raphael's assistant Giulio Romano (then living in Mantua only a day's ride from Vicenza), of Serlio's master Peruzzi, and of Sanmicheli's colleague Antonio da Sangallo the Younger.

13 Palladio: the contrasting plain gable wall and ornamental entrance serliana of the Villa Valmarana at Vigardolo, after 1541.

This first visit to Rome was a revelation to Palladio. He later wrote in his *Quattro libri* that he found the ancient buildings 'much more worthy of observation than at first I had imagined', and the 'enormous ruins' greatly moved him. This took some imagination and enthusiasm. The remains were usually buried by accumulated alluvium or centuries of debris (the Forum was known as the 'Campo Vaccino', the cowfield, since it was used for pasture), or were absorbed into later buildings, making surveying difficult and reconstruction drawings necessary. Palladio persisted, as the evidence of many surviving drawings from this and later trips shows.

Immediately on his return to Vicenza, he was presented with more important commissions which provided him with an early opportunity to apply the lessons of Rome. His design work for the Villa Valmarana at Vigardolo is indicative of the instruction he had received from Trissino and Cornaro, overlaid by his first impressions of Rome. Outwardly, the villa is almost barn-like in appearance, with ornament confined to the doors and windows, but internally spaces are vaulted and reflect the influence of the ancient

13

Roman baths he had seen. The elegant simplicity and unadorned wall surfaces seem to reflect Cornaro's view that not every building requires a profusion of ornament to be classical: 'A building may well be beautiful, and comfortable, and be neither Doric nor of any such order.' The arched entrance motif with its triple openings derives from designs by Bramante and Raphael, but was taken up by Serlio and is reproduced in many of his published designs, so that it became known as a 'serliana' (though in England and America it was to be called a 'Palladian window' or 'Venetian window').

At a formal level, Palladio's designs became simpler and less reliant on the individual formulas of other architects. The sequence of drawings for the Villa Pisani at Bagnolo reveals a search for a personal 14 vocabulary which is characterized by bold spatial manipulations such as a great entrance hemicycle, which may have been inspired by Roman baths, Trajan's Market, Bramante's Belvedere Court in the Vatican or perhaps the built portion of Raphael's Villa Madama. The feature was abandoned at Bagnolo, but something like it reappears in the designs for the Villa Mocenigo at Dolo, with extravagant double 15 curving wings (of which a reduced version was built, only to be demolished in the 19th century). The Villa Pisani design has a central cruciform main room or *sala*, which is barrel-vaulted and lit by thermal windows (tripartite semi-circular openings so called because they are common features of Roman *thermae* or baths). Like the sweeping curved forecourt, this type of space recurs in his later villas.

In the villas where the house is made distinct from the farm buildings (the latter being arranged within the wings which are linked with the living accommodation by colonnades), the hierarchy of form that resulted emphasized the status of the activities within. This worked well in the open landscape setting of the villa. With the palace, because urban plots were so dense, the surface of the façade, not the silhouette of the building, characterized the site and its occupants. Behind this comes a sequence of closely knit spaces, organized around open courts which are used to provide adequate daylight and ventilation, and the settings for interior rooms. The first of the new palaces in Vicenza to integrate plan, façade and courtyard convincingly was the Palazzo Thiene. 16,17

There is confusion as to the precise nature of Palladio's involvement with the Palazzo Thiene: he claims it as his own, but his successor Vincenzo Scamozzi later asserted that Giulio Romano (1492/9–1546) was the designer. Giulio had arrived in Vicenza from Mantua in December 1542 as yet another consultant for the decrepit Palazzo

14   Palladio: a preliminary elevation and plan for the Villa Pisani, Bagnolo, 1542.

16, 17   *opposite* Giulio Romano(?) and Palladio: Palazzo Thiene, Vicenza, 1542–58. Plan and section from the *Quattro libri*, Book II, and façade.

15   *below* Palladio: presentation drawing of the plan and elevation of the Villa Mocenigo at Dolo, mid–1550s, as published in the *Quattro libri*, Book II.

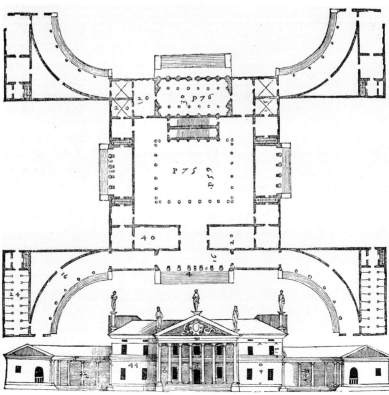

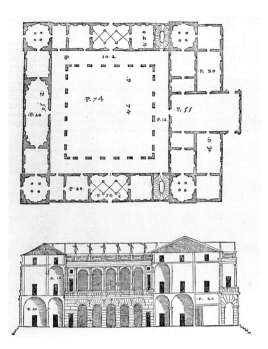

della Ragione. There can be no doubting his eminence and suitability. He had been Raphael's chief assistant in Rome and then architect to the Gonzaga court in Mantua, where between 1527 and 1534 he had built the celebrated Palazzo del Te. Consequently his arrival in Vicenza was something of an occasion, with high expectations to match the substantial fee he inevitably commanded: 50 gold *scudi* for a two-week visit.

It is conceivable that Giulio was invited to design the palace. The 16,17 Thiene had contacts with the Gonzaga court (Isabella Gonzaga was married to Teodoro Thiene), and it was probably their suggestion that brought Giulio an invitation to Vicenza from the Council. The palace as built conforms with Giulio's general architectural approach elsewhere, though there are differences, particularly in details above the ground floor. It has been conjectured that only the lower storey had been built by the time of Giulio's death, and that Palladio, who was identified merely as a stonemason at the witnessing of the building contract in 1542, succeeded him. It seems less likely that Palladio had been given such an important commission outright, as he was little known and untested. His rise to fame was imminent, however: the Thiene contract helped, raising his prestige, and the family may have promoted him as a local candidate able to resolve the problem of the Palazzo della Ragione.

According to the minute book of the City Council, Giulio's advice about the Palazzo della Ragione was expedient and took account of what had survived of the earlier structure. The core was to be left alone. The surrounding colonnade was to be strengthened by encasing the supports in stone piers which would also replace the part that had collapsed. In addition, Giulio proposed that the ground around the building should be levelled so that the Palazzo would appear 'planted in the middle of a piazza, which should be surrounded by porticoes like a cloister'. This idea was never pursued, though the principle of encasing the existing Gothic core was adopted, once a further period of vacillation was overcome and problems of detail settled.

18   Just prior to his first trip to Rome in 1541, Palladio had been sketching ideas for this building himself, and on 5 March 1546 he submitted a design to the Council, in association with the Pedemuro workshop. The Council responded positively and authorized the construction of a full-size trial bay in wood. Palladio's succession to Giulio Romano here (and probably at the Palazzo Thiene as well) should not be misconstrued. He may have been required to, or may have chosen to, assimilate some of the ideas of his celebrated predecessor – indeed predecessors – for this project, but it required great skill and knowledge of the classical vocabulary to produce a satisfactory building *all'antica*, and there were some awkward inconsistencies in the existing structure which had to be overcome, and which substantially affected the final outcome. The main problem was that the existing bays were irregular in width, which precluded the simple modular repetition of an arcade; their spacing was too great, however, for a trabeated system. Once an arched solution was adopted, intervening piers were required to conceal any dimensional irregularities, and to maintain a constant level for the springing-points and the tops of the arches, which was necessary to ensure a coincidence with the existing loggia vaults. As Palladio's first proposal suggests, such piers would have been broad and heavy, and would have prevented light from penetrating deep enough at ground level. Since there were rented commercial units here which provided the Council with an income, this would have been impractical.

19,21,22   Palladio's eventual resolution of these problems was brilliantly simple. He proposed that the piers should be composed of separate

32

18   Palladio: an early proposal for the Basilica, Vicenza, c. 1540. The openings appear equally spaced; the orders are paired, whereas the final design is articulated by single half-columns (Ill. 22).

elements. The main framework is a trabeated system of applied half-columns supporting entablatures, Doric below and Ionic above. Laced between is an arcuated system supported on a smaller order of Doric and Ionic columns. The eye is drawn to the regularly spaced arched openings, and the trabeated frame is interpreted as regularly spaced too, since discrepancies in bay widths are adjusted by means of the gaps between the two systems – that is, between the columns supporting the arched openings, arranged as serlianas, and the solid piers.

An illustration in Serlio's Book IV (1537) shows a Doric arcaded system with an Ionic arrangement above in the form of serlianas with oculi in the spandrels similar to those Palladio used, and this illustration is often cited as a model to which Palladio may have referred; but since it was published over a year before Serlio's own official visit to Vicenza, he may have provided the Council with a similar design, and that may be what Palladio knew. Sansovino's proposal for the Basilica may have been a scheme derived from his Library of St Mark's, which is similarly two storeys high and

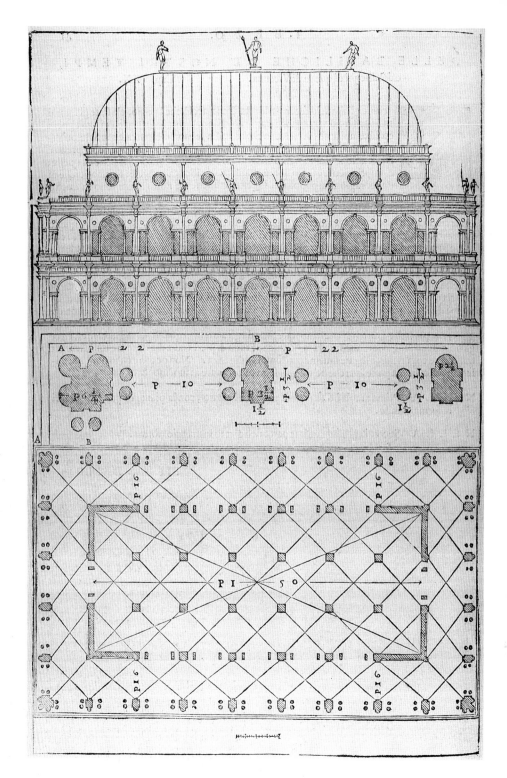

his reaction, no harmonization of systems was attempted; and in any case Italians had become adept at translating measures from one place to another. To perform any commercial transaction between different systems formulae provided by the Merchant's Key or the Rule of Three were generally used. These involved an interaction of means and extremes which was familiar to any recipient of a basic education, and which made the process of proportioning a building design quite straightforward.

Alberti used a proportional procedure to explain the numbers behind the classical orders (IX, 7, pp. 309ff.): the first columns were 6 and 10 units high, but these were rejected as either too thick or too slender, and the ancients sought a column that 'lay between the two extremes. They therefore resorted first to arithmetic, added the two together, and then divided the sum in half; by this they established that the number that lay between 6 and 10 was 8. This pleased them, and they made a column 8 times the width of the base, and called it Ionic.' Alberti applies this same procedure to determine the Doric canon as 7 modules high $(6 + 8 = 14 \div 2 = 7)$ and the Corinthian as 9 modules $(8 + 10 = 18 \div 2 = 9)$.

Alberti had written on the relationship between musical theory and the 'ideal' ratios for architecture in the chapter preceding his discussion of the orders. The formula of the mean and two extremes was applied to the sequence of the Pythagorean harmonic scale which was known to every humanist artist and architect. The argument Alberti put for the appropriateness of musical theory to architecture was that 'The very same numbers that cause sounds to have that *concinnitas* [a certain harmony] pleasing to the ears, can also fill the eyes and mind with wondrous delight' (p. 305). The sentiment was echoed by Palladio in his *Quattro libri*. The Greek harmonic system is determined by the relationship of four similar strings, of a proportionally related length, expressible as the progression 6:8:9:12. Pythagoras found that when these strings are vibrated, under equal tension, the sound (wave length) interval between them creates consonant tones, which correspond to ratios of whole numbers. Doubling the string length (1:2) creates an octave (called by the Greeks *diapason*); a ratio of 2:3 creates a difference in pitch of a fifth (*diapente*); of 3:4 creates a fourth (*diatessaron*). Again, as Alberti explains,

the musical numbers are 1, 2, 3 and 4; there is also *tonus* where the longer string is one eighth more than the lesser. Architects employ all these numbers in the most convenient manner possible: they use them in pairs, as in laying out a forum, *piazza*, or open space, where only two dimensions are considered, width and length; and they use them also in threes, such as a public sitting room, senate house, hall, and so on, when width relates to length, and they want the height to relate harmoniously to both.

These 'perfect' numbers can be found in the plans that Palladio published late in his career in the *Quattro libri*. They occur either singly or, more usually, as ratios determining the harmonious arrangement of the principal elements. In realizing these proportional systems, expressed in whole numbers, Palladio habitually used the measurements of the locality in which he was working. He could hardly do otherwise, since the local measures determined the size of his building materials, such as bricks. He would have used the Vicentine foot (357mm) in and around Vicenza, and the slightly shorter Venetian foot (348mm) in Venice.

When he came to publish the plans of ancient Roman buildings, however, he was faced with the difficulty that the Roman foot was shorter than either of these measurements (about 296mm), so there could be no precise correspondences in their proportions. Had he kept the measurements of Roman buildings in Roman feet these correspondences would have been clear, but he chose to convert them into Vicentine feet, and their proportional relationships were thus obscured. They could no longer be expressed in terms of 'perfect' numbers, or indeed of whole numbers at all. The result was that while the proportional systems of his own buildings were recognizable, those of the antique buildings (and of highly regarded Renaissance buildings of 'perfection' like Bramante's Tempietto), which were equally carefully calculated, were overlooked. The more popular the *Quattro libri*, with its dimensions in Vicentine feet, became, the more this unfortunate consequence increased. In the end, paradoxically, this contributed to the devaluing of number and measure in architecture as elements bearing a universal significance, and to their becoming merely expressions of quantity.

Palladio designed with preferred numbers which are multiples of the local foot familiar to his masons. Brick dimensions were determined by the foot; and repetitive elements, such as column shafts, could be ordered in standard sizes from the quarry, a practice common in ancient Rome and Venice itself. Room dimensions are often multiples and combinations of the numbers 6, 10 and 16, which become design modules of a sort: rooms are typically 6 × 10 feet, 10 × 16, 16 × 16, 16 × 26½ (an approximation of the ratio 6:10 – not, as is sometimes said, 3:5). They can also be based on harmonic numbers and combinations: typically 12 × 18, 18 × 18, 18 × 27, 18 × 30, etc. Overlaps occur between the two systems.

With Alberti's notion of *concinnitas*, number, measure and proportion are the means by which architectural space is made to conform with natural principles. Palladio too was adamant that such principles should be followed, and he expressed forcibly his dissatisfaction with 'that manner of building, which departs from that which Nature teaches us about things, and from that simplicity which one discerns in those things created by her, almost creates another Nature and departs from the true, good, and beautiful way of building' (I, p. 51).

The secrets of Nature had been explored in the 'natural' architecture of antiquity, and Christian commentators had long been fascinated by the Biblical archetypes – Noah's Ark, Solomon's Temple and Palace complex – which exhibited certain natural numerical and proportional combinations, and had anthropomorphic parallels too (such as the relationship of the Ark to human proportions described by Alberti above, following St Augustine). All this is behind Palladio's belief that buildings 'should appear an entire, and well finished body' (I, 6); later in the same book he relates the hierarchy of space and use within a building to the body: just as 'our blessed Lord had designed the parts of our body, so that the most beautiful should be in places which are exposed to sight and the less decent in hidden places', so there should be noble spaces, and concealed areas of utility within buildings. Consequently, kitchens were placed below with the cellar, or in some villas in outbuildings along with stables and storerooms; whereas the principal living and entertaining rooms in both the villas and the palaces were placed on the ground and first floors. In the villas the roof space was often used as a granary.

If the outside of a building should appear like a 'well finished body' and expressive of this hierarchy of use, the organization of the interior spaces should also be arranged hierarchically, the whole and the parts being resolved through the application of geometry and proportion. For the interior Palladio described seven room shapes as the finest and most successful: 'they are either made round (though rarely) or square, or their length will be the diagonal line of the square, or of a square and a third, or of one square and a half, or of one square and two thirds, or of two squares' (I, 21). Ideally, the height of a room is to be determined by a harmonic sequence, though, as he admits, 'it will

41

not be possible always to find this height in whole numbers'; 'there are also other heights for vaults, which do not come under any rule, and are therefore left for the architect to make use of as necessity requires, and according to his own judgment' (cf. Burlington and Chiswick Villa, below, p. 165). He offers two examples for scrutiny. First, using the formula of height equals the square root of length times width: 'if the place that we intend to vault is 9 feet long, and 4 wide, the height of the vault will be 6 feet; and the same proportion that 9 has to 6, 6 also has to 4, that is *sesquialteral*.' The second example is arranged thus:

length	*height*	*breadth*	
12	9	6	the height, 9, is found by halving the sum of the length and the breadth, thus: $12 + 6 = 18$; $18 \div 2 = 9$
108	72	54	the median number, 9, multiplies the extremes, 12 and 6, thus: $9 \times 12 = 108$; $9 \times 6 = 54$
	8		72 is found by multiplying the extremes, 12×6. 8 is the number that multiplies 9 to equal 72

What Palladio wished to show here was a number which is proportionable to the harmonic sequence, but allows flexibility if it be necessary to have a lower vaulted ceiling (say to maintain a uniform floor covering above), ensuring that it will remain 'beautiful to the eye'. This is typical of his approach, which is in contrast to the more uncompromising doctrine of Vitruvius and Alberti. Palladio states the 'ideal' objectives and the principles that will obtain them, yet he offers simplified and practical methods for achieving 'similar' results, in the light of his own considerable experience, which allowed him to pare down the 'laws of Nature' to the essentials required by architects.

There can be no doubting the missionary zeal with which, by the early 1550s, he was intent on spreading the Vitruvian classical message, for several publications were in hand which he produced alone or in collaboration, and which were intended to clarify and so promote the course he himself had embarked on. The most important of these early publications was a new edition of Vitruvius's treatise produced with Daniele Barbaro, which grew out of an architectural collaboration with Daniele and his brother Marc'Antonio on their new villa at Maser.

In Vicenza, early in September 1548, after the wooden mock-up for
the Basilica by Palladio had been built, three civic commissioners
were selected to supervise the building project. They authorized
payment to Palladio for more drawings and models, though his
involvement long-term was still in the balance. Models of earlier
schemes had been ordered, made, and abandoned. The decision to
proceed was not made until a full Council debate on 11 April 1549,
when the commissioners offered persuasive arguments in favour of
Palladio's design. It won the day, by a vote of 99 to 17. Palladio was
appointed superintendent immediately and work began the following month. Although not completed in his lifetime, the Basilica was
of major importance for his subsequent involvement with public
architecture.

Palladio had many noble friends in that decisive debate who had
already committed themselves to his architecture. Pietro Godi, whose
villa at Lonedo was the first that Palladio designed, was an obvious
rallying-point for support. Most influential for the debate, however,
were Gian Alvise Valmarana and Girolamo Chiericati, two of the
building commissioners, whose families were current patrons of
Palladio and who individually patronized him, and Gabriele Capra,
who was civic supervisor for the timber mock-up of the sample bay.

Girolamo Chiericati had Palladio design him a palace at about this
time (*c.* 1550). It is a two-storeyed U-shaped building which forms   25
a courtyard to the rear, while along the front there is a two-tier
colonnaded portico. When Girolamo asked for permission to build
the portico, which actually projected beyond his site, he pleaded
successfully that it would be 'for my greater convenience and for the
convenience and ornament of the whole city', since it fronted a piazza
used as Vicenza's cattle market and offered a distinguished backdrop
and a place to shelter nobles who frequented it.

The portico, eleven bays long, is Doric at ground level and Ionic
above, with a central element of five bays set slightly proud of three-
bay-long wings. The Doric entablature follows an example by
Sanmicheli, and the arches that close the ends at both levels derive
from the antique Portico of Octavia in Rome (see below, p. 84). The   65
upper storey has its central element walled in, to provide the
Chiericati with private accommodation.

43

23   Serlio: Poggio Reale, from Book III, 1540/1619.

24   An early drawing for the palace (which differs in a number of respects from the final building) shows the projecting centre emphasized by a pediment. Serlio's influence may have been felt here, 23   since it resembles an elevation he had published in Book III (1540, pp. 122–23). Houses with pediments – an allusion to the antique temple front – were relatively uncommon in the Renaissance. The Villa Medici at Poggio a Caiano, to the west of Florence, by Giuliano da Sangallo, was the first to display such a 'temple front' on its façade; it acquired its present form in the 1480s. Palladio, or the Chiericati, decided against building the pediment here; but the 'temple' motif was to be used frequently by Palladio in his villa architecture. His reasons for adopting it probably came from his association with the Barbaro brothers who, after Trissino's death in 1550, helped him to consolidate his theory of architecture and devoted much of their energy to promoting his proven talent.

44

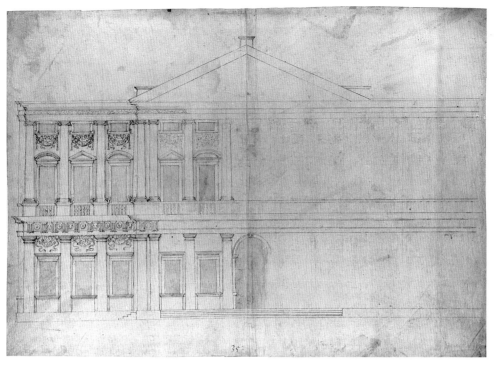

24 Palladio: project for the Palazzo Chiericati, Vicenza, *c.* 1550.

25 Palladio: Palazzo Chiericati, Vicenza, *c.* 1550–57, seen across the former cattle market.

26 Portrait of Daniele Barbaro
attributed to Paolo Veronese.
He is holding his edition of
Vitruvius (1556); behind is his
treatise on perspective (1568).

26   Daniele and Marc'Antonio Barbaro were an extraordinarily gifted pair. Daniele (1514–70) was a noted Aristotelian scholar and diplomat. Between 1549 and 1551 he represented Venice in England and Scotland; on his return he was rewarded for his services with the title of Patriarch Elect of Aquileia, which provided him with an income, but precluded him from holding public office. His brother, Marc'Antonio (1518–95), became a leading Venetian statesman, and promoted Palladio in Venice. Both men were concerned with good design. Daniele was probably responsible for the layout of the Botanical Gardens in Padua, and Palladio later credited Marc' Antonio with the invention of a cantilevered staircase (I, 28).

     Palladio may have started to design a villa for the brothers in 1549. We know he travelled with Daniele to Trent in 1552 and Rome in 1554, and he must also have begun to work with him on an important new edition of Vitruvius in those years, as it was published in 1556. It was with both brothers that he collaborated at Maser.

27,28   The Villa Barbaro stands on the slope of a low hill, and its structure incorporates the existing family *castello*. The central accommodation block follows the general form of the old castle: Palladio's *piano nobile* roughly coincides with the *soler* and the new attics with the old third floor, as is shown by the medieval fireplaces still concealed within the fabric. Palladio extended the first floor of the villa back towards the hill, where he formed an open terrace area and a semi-circular *nymphaeum* which collected water from the natural spring behind. The

46

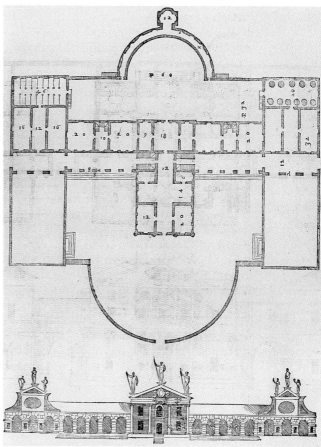

27, 28 Palladio:
Villa Barbaro, Maser,
c. 1550–58. View, and
plan and elevation from
the *Quattro libri*, Book II.
The *nymphaeum* is cut into
the slope behind at the
level of the *piano nobile*.

ingenious section of this structure may have been inspired by a preview of Serlio's ideas on building on sloping sites and on utilizing natural springs (published in Book VII in 1575). Both architects may, however, have been influenced by Raphael's Villa Madama in Rome, where there was a pool and fountain, described by Raphael as 'cut out of the hill in a semicircle'. Marc'Antonio has been credited with the design and sculpting of the building's ornament, though the sculptor Alessandro Vittoria and the painter Paolo Veronese (who complemented the architecture and sculpture in the villa with brilliant illusionistic frescoes) were active contributors of their art, so that the final outcome is a blend of many ideas and talents.

Daniele, for his part, may well have brought to this venture a clear set of directives and the programme for the villa. He was the undoubted expert on classical philosophy, though he probably lacked the knowledge of antique architecture that Palladio had gained. Their trip to Rome together in 1554 may have enabled Daniele to become acquainted with some of the monuments and details with which Palladio was now familiar. Such experience would have been invaluable for their work together on the new *Vitruvius* as well as the
3   villa project. Modern buildings like the Villa Madama, or the Villa Giulia (1550–55) that Pope Julius III was having built just outside the city walls, may have been part of their itinerary, since the Villa Barbaro seems to refer to formal aspects of both.

They probably also caught sight of the designs Pirro Ligorio had made for Cardinal Ippolito d'Este for a villa and terraced water gardens at Tivoli, and his villa on the slopes of the Quirinal, since meetings took place between the architects and their patrons. Palladio compared drawings of antique monuments with Ligorio, and interpreted his drawings of the so-called 'Temple of Clitumnus', the
54 Roman villa at Anguillara, and Palestrina; Ligorio copied Palladio's drawings of sites he had not surveyed, such as the Porta Aurea at Ravenna and the amphitheatre at Verona. There are new drawings by Palladio from this trip as well, with general plans and sections of the
29 Baths of Agrippa and detailed studies of its ornament. Daniele and the Cardinal may have discussed the Barbaro *Vitruvius*: writing was probably well advanced by this time, so that a *viva voce* with Ippolito d'Este, who was knowledgeable about Roman antiquities, would have assisted Daniele greatly. When the book was published in 1556 it was dedicated to the Cardinal.

Daniele's interpretation of Vitruvius was informed by his Aristotelian training at the University of Padua. In 1544, four years after

48

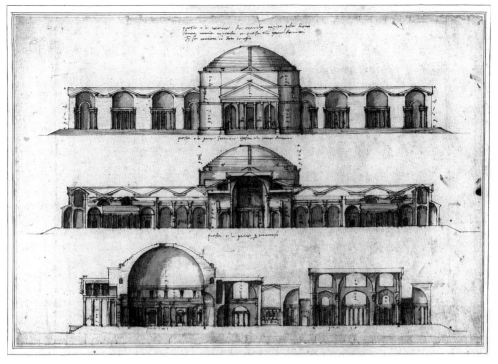

29 Palladio: reconstruction of the Baths of Agrippa and the Pantheon, Rome, in elevation, longitudinal section, and cross-section, mid-1550s.

graduating, he published two books on Aristotle's writings: a commentary on the *Rhetoric* (accompanying a Latin translation by his great-uncle Ermolao Barbaro), and an edition of the *Nicomachean Ethics*. On the basis of a passage in the *Ethics*, he decreed that painting, sculpture and architecture rely on five qualities defined by Aristotle: Arts, Science, Prudence, Intellect and Wisdom. According to Barbaro's argument, the Arts are founded on a proper understanding of Nature which can only be revealed by direct experience. Experience is the combination of thought and action, regulated by Prudence and Intellect which direct the individual to Wisdom. Science comes from experience, and also from the application of Intellect: the intellect is used to establish definite 'proofs' which lead to understanding and certain 'truths'. The certainties of Science are balanced by the uncertainties of the Arts, which do not reflect 'truths' but individual determination to imitate natural order (through the mastery of number, geometry and mathematics). Only the Intellect is

49

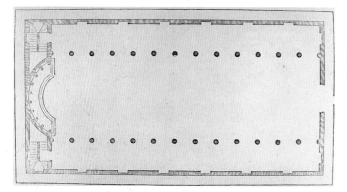

30 Reconstruction of the plan of an antique basilica, from Book V of the Barbaro *Vitruvius*, 1556.

truly innate and, as such, is variable, being determined by the strength and *virtù* of the creative artist. It was out of this definition of the Arts that Barbaro's concern for architecture sprang, because to his way of thinking neither of the other two arts can represent the virtues more comprehensively.

Palladio agreed with this, detecting in the ruins of Rome 'a shining and sublime testimony of Roman *virtù* and grandeur', the very qualities to which Daniele referred in his edition of *Vitruvius*. Palladio contributed his experience of antiquity which he interpreted through drawings of the main building types described by Vitruvius. These illustrations almost certainly gave the text a much wider appeal than Daniele's words alone would have had. Palladio drew plans and partial sections and elevations of the principal public buildings: the

30,31,76 basilica, Greek and Roman theatres, the palaestra (a porticoed enclosure for 'philosophical disputation', as Alberti put it), and the 'perfect' temple form. The designs which illustrate the text, like the ruins he had studied in Rome, were 'proofs' of a natural architecture, which he subsequently realized as 'truths' in his own buildings. Consequently, Palladio's collaboration with Barbaro was of fundamental importance to the future maturity of his architecture.

A frequent feature of Palladio's later work, the temple portico, which he grafts onto the villa form, is an example of a 'proof' subsequently becoming an architectural 'truth' or reality. This

32–34 element appears in the reconstruction of the 'House of the Ancients' in Book VI of the Barbaro *Vitruvius* (pp. 278–81). The plan and part section show a rectangular building with a central courtyard, of which the general scheme is in fact based on the Palazzo Farnese in Rome, begun by Antonio da Sangallo the Younger (and completed after his death in 1546 by Michelangelo). The Barbaro elevation, with its giant pedimented portico, is less obviously derived from a single

50

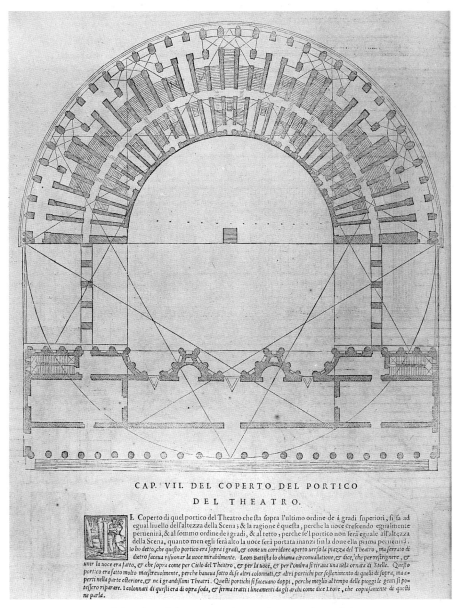

31   Reconstruction of the plan of the Roman theatre, from Book V of the Barbaro *Vitruvius*, 1556. Four equilateral triangles determine the positions of the staircases, the semi-circle of seating, and the openings in the stage backdrop, called the *scaenae frons*. In the text Vitruvius is describing the roof of the colonnade above the uppermost seats, which should be proportioned so as to trap effectively the voices of the actors below.

building. There is, however, a clear basis for it in the theory he developed from Vitruvius.

Vitruvius (II, 1) described the pediment as an element derived from the gable end construction of the earliest forms of dwelling house, where men

set up forked stakes connected by twigs and covered these walls with mud. Others made walls of lumps of dried mud, covering them with reeds and leaves to keep out the rain and the heat. Finding that such roofs could not stand the rain during the storms of winter, they built them with peaks daubed with mud, the roofs sloping and projecting so as to carry off the rainwater.

Later, in the *Quattro libri*, Palladio reasoned that the primitive house evolved, as society matured, into public buildings: 'of several houses, villages were formed, and then of many villages, cities, and in these public places and buildings were made' (Preface); and these grander buildings had impressive pediments. This 'evolutionary' argument was important for Palladio, because Alberti had expressed concern that, for reasons of propriety, 'the pediment to a private house should not emulate the majesty of a temple in any way' (IX, 4, p. 301). Palladio, by reasoning that the pediment of the temple was derived from the house, disarmed such criticism: 'The ancients also made use of [pediments] in their buildings, as is seen in the remains of the temples, and other public edifices, and they probably took the invention and the principles [of them] from private buildings, i.e. from the houses' (II, 16).

If the house-type developed into the more perfect temple-type, Palladio also considered the house to be the model for the city – a

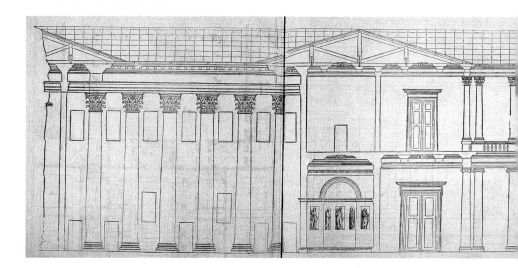

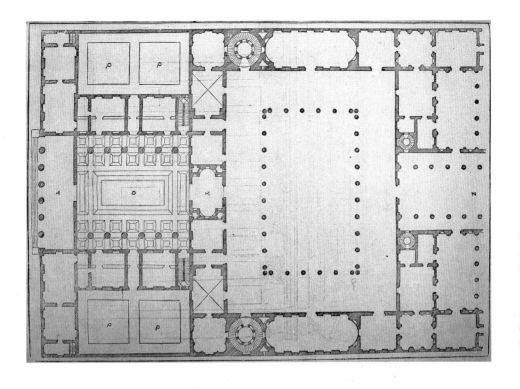

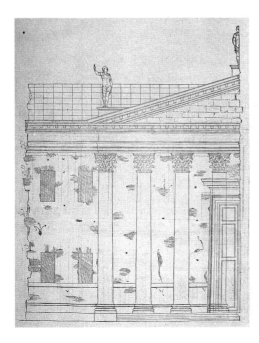

32–34 Reconstruction of the 'House of the Ancients', from Book VI of the Barbaro *Vitruvius*, 1556: section through the entrance court, vestibule and part of the main courtyard (*opposite*), plan (the entrance portico is at the left), and part elevation of the entrance portico. Note the varied shapes of the rooms surrounding the larger courtyard (cf. Ills. 16, 121, 127).

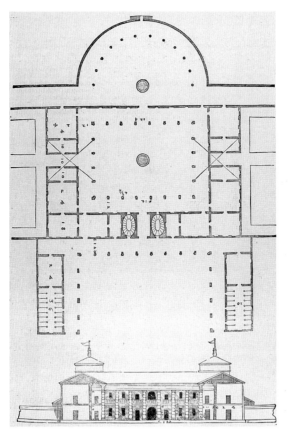

35 Palladio: plan and
sectional elevation
through the U-shaped
entry court of the
Villa Serego at Santa
Sofia, built between
1565 and 1569, from
the *Quattro libri*,
Book II.

notion he borrowed from Alberti: 'the city is as it were but a great
house, and, on the contrary, the country house is a little city' (*Quattro
libri*, II, 12). Alberti related this house-city, city-house relationship
more fully: 'If (as the philosophers maintain) the city is like some large
house, and the house is in turn like a small city, cannot the various
parts of the house – atria, *xysti* [open colonnaded spaces for
promenading], dining rooms, porticoes, and so on – be considered
miniature buildings?' (*Ten Books*, I, 9, p. 23). This line of thinking was
influential for Palladio's development of the villa form. Palladio
designed two principal types of villas: those where the elements of the
'house' could be separated out as distinct forms and arranged
hierarchically, with the principal accommodation at the centre,
flanked by 'dependencies' (kitchens, stables, etc.), of which the Villa
Barbaro is an obvious example; and those arranged as a single large

28

block around a courtyard – as buildings might be placed around a forum, with the emphasis on enclosed space rather than on the structures as a series of objects – which is how the Villa Serego at Santa Sofia, one of his last, was planned.   35

The second type of villa – the inward-looking house – owes much to Palladio's formulation of the House of the Ancients. This model   32,33 was suitable, too, for an urban setting, and is evident in Palladio's palace designs from the mid-1550s onwards. The earlier Palazzo Thiene ground floor plan, perhaps by Giulio Romano, was derived   16 from Bramante's design for the Palazzo dei Tribunali in Rome, which, with its four emphasized corners and square central courtyard, reflects the geometrical configuration of Giuliano da Sangallo's villa at Poggio a Caiano. Two of Palladio's later projects in Vicenza, for the Palazzo da Porto Festa (of the late 1540s) and Palazzo Barbarano   70 (which may date from the early 1550s, although the design was revised and construction continued into the 1570s), derive their internal clarity from regularly shaped atrium spaces, which in some of the designs for Palazzo Barbarano are covered to maximize the internal space on the site. However, whereas the Palazzo Thiene was planned with its accommodation all around the courtyard, these later palaces are more constricted, with rooms on only two opposite sides of the central open space.

A 'house' in Venice, the Convent of the Carità, a project   36 commissioned from Palladio by the Lateran Canons in 1560, is a more complex interpretation of the House of the Ancients. The demands of accommodating a community rather than a household called for a varied sequence of spaces, which Palladio adapted from the intricate planning of Roman baths, though the overall form of the design is very true to its Vitruvian model, with its hierarchy of primary open courtyards flanked symmetrically by rooms of various sizes and proportions. Only part of the complex was built and that was damaged by fire in 1630, yet the scale and the exposed brickwork of what remains still suggest the magnificent constructional boldness of the baths, stripped in their ruined state to their brick and concrete core. This massiveness is tempered in the courtyard, which has finely proportioned superimposed orders and ornamented openings that model the bare brickwork and provide a human scale appropriate to a 'house'.

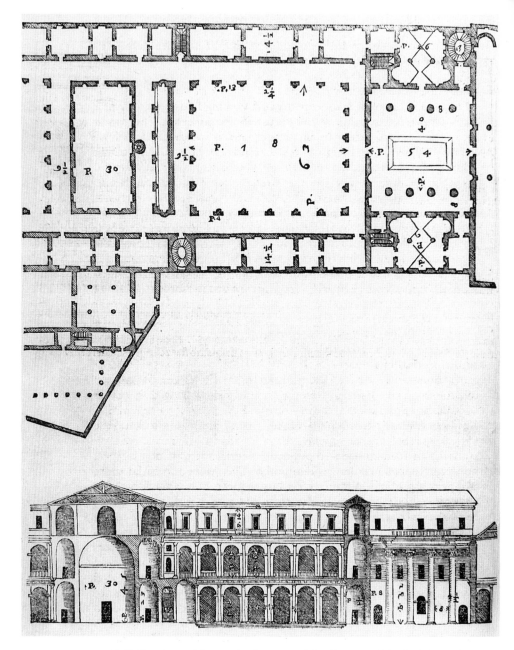

36 Palladio: plan and longitudinal section of the Convent of the Carità, Venice, 1560–70, from the *Quattro libri*, Book II.

The importance of the Carità to Palladio's career can hardly be   36
overstated. It was his first major commission in Venice, the city that
he held in the highest regard architecturally in the region, since it was
the only 'surviving example of the greatness and magnificence of the
Romans' (I, p. 5). His ambition to contribute to this centre of
excellence and not to remain a provincial architect had been evident in
his application six years earlier, in 1554, to become *proto* of the Salt
Magistracy, the state agency behind all Venetian public works.
Moreover, the job was salaried and would have provided the security
and regular income he had not enjoyed for over a decade – ever since
he had left the Pedemuro workshop. Although Palladio probably
received the influential support of Daniele Barbaro, and had a number
of important commissions to his name already in the provinces, he
was not appointed. Why his application was unsuccessful is not
known, but perhaps it was his very success in Vicenza and the support
he received from the Vicentine nobles that lay behind his initial
rejection for public office in Venice.

Although Vicenza had been part of the Venetian Republic since
1404, the wars of the League of Cambrai, after 1508, which aimed to
cancel out a century of Venetian expansion on the mainland, showed
the tensions that existed between the two cities. During this conflict
Vicenza sided against Venice in favour of the Holy Roman Empire,
and a Vicentine nobleman, with the support of fellow nobles and the
encouragement of the citizens, marched into Vicenza with eighty
Austrian mercenaries. After only about a decade of independence,
however, Venetian rule was reimposed. This proved to be far more
stringent than before: the city's disloyalty was not easily forgotten,
and even in the next century Vicentine nobles were still considered to
be untrustworthy.

Gian Giorgio Trissino was not exempted from this prejudice. He
had shown enthusiastic support for the new Habsburg Emperor,
Charles V, whose coronation he had attended in 1519. Trissino's
expression of this allegiance was long-lasting, for in 1547 he dedicated
his *L'Italia liberata dai Gotthi* – the epic poem in which 'Palladio'
appeared – to Charles V. The dedication suggests that Trissino wished
Charles to regard himself as the second Justinian who would come
from the West to liberate the East from the infidel Turks. The promise
of such an adventure had been the excuse for the League of Cambrai in

the first place, so that Venetians were unlikely to have applauded Trissinian sentiments here.

Other noble families who were Palladio's patrons held radically divergent views of the religious upheaval taking place just over the Alps. Ever since Martin Luther nailed his paper of 95 theses to the door of the castle church at Wittenberg in Saxony, in 1517, the role of the Roman Catholic Church had been scrutinized more critically. The enduring message of Luther, that individual men were responsible only to God, not to the authority of the Church, revolutionized northern European religious action, but its impact was monitored and suppressed in the Papal States.

As a great trading centre Venice was one of the first cities to receive the printed word of Lutheran doctrine, but the influence of this revolution was felt most forcibly through the migration to Switzerland of second-generation Protestants who sought refuge there from Catholic persecution, in a haven created by the French-born John Calvin: in the decade after 1549 some five thousand Protestants settled in Geneva, and their growing numbers and proximity to northern Italy posed a threat of which papal Rome was aware.

In northern Italy around the 1540s *la Riforma*, the Reformation, was especially prevalent in Vicenza and Bologna. Vicenza harboured radical supporters of the Church and heretics. At one extreme there were staunch Catholics such as the Vicentine nobleman Gaetano Thiene (1480–1547), who, with the Neapolitan Gian Piero Carafa (1476–1559), formed the Theatines, a new order of clergy and laity heavily committed to pastoral care. Their direct involvement with the people and the personal zeal of Carafa to oppose the Lutheran threat led to his appointment in 1542 as Inquisitor-General. His success at rooting out heretics was rewarded when he became pope, as Paul IV, in 1555. His efforts were influential and a General Council of the Catholic Church was convened to confront the Lutheran threat. Vicenza was an early meeting point, before the Council's most effective phase at the more neutral Trent, an Italian city ruled by the Holy Roman Empire. Here in 1564 new legislation was enacted which strengthened the powers of the bishops and their pastoral ministry. The Inquisition rooted out any opposition to the established Church, and nobody was exempt from their scrutiny, irrespective of social standing.

In Vicenza, prominent Vicentines were identified as heretics. The finger was pointed at two of Palladio's patrons, Francesco Repeta and Francesco Thiene, and the Inquisition investigated them. They were accused of holding gatherings every Saturday, alternately at their respective villas at Campiglia and Cicogna, though these they claimed were no more than meetings for the 'reading and interpreting of Petrarch's sonnets'. Although the charges were dropped, official suspicion of the Repeta family continued, and Francesco's son Mario was denounced in 1569 as a 'Despiser of the Church and of masses', though, again, this allegation was unproven. The villa which Palladio designed for Francesco, and which Mario finished building, was as unconventional as the family: it was a simple single-storey barn-like building, U-shaped around a court. The *Quattro libri* illustration shows its horizontal emphasis relieved by a low pediment and corner dovecote-towers. The rooms in the range opposite the stables had specific dedications – some 'to continence, others to justice, and others to other virtues, with elogiums [short inscriptions] and paintings adapted to the subject'. This demarcation of space allowed Mario Repeta to 'lodge his visitors and friends in the rooms inscribed to that virtue to which he thinks them mostly inclined' (II, 15).

37

37   Palladio: plan and sectional elevation of the Villa Repeta, Campiglia, designed *c.* 1557 and under construction in 1566, from the *Quattro libri*, Book II.

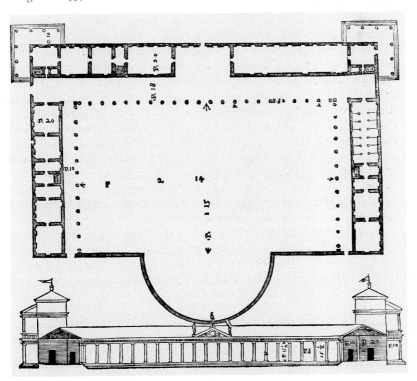

Whilst Gian Giorgio Trissino was not a Lutheran, his son, Giulio, was identified with the heretics. This put his position as Archpriest of the Cathedral in Vicenza in serious jeopardy. Giulio's cousin Alessandro Trissino was actually arrested for heresy, but escaped to Calvin's Geneva where he remained out of reach of the Catholic Church – whose authority he likened to the 'bonds of the devil'. Another noble who chose exile was Odoardo Thiene, with whom Palladio was connected closely. He was a central figure in two academies concerned with religious reform, and as the Inquisition closed in he left voluntarily for Geneva in the late 1560s, and became a citizen there in 1576.

The intellectual liberty of Vicenza was constrained by the Inquisition and the Venetians. When independently minded Vicentines struggled against this, the Church responded with the threat of the Inquisition, and Venice penalized the city through an onerous financial levy. To ensure that Vicenza complied, as in other mainland Venetian cities there was a resident Venetian *capitano*, a military commander, whose offices were just across the Piazza dei Signori from the Palazzo della Ragione in the predecessor of the present Loggia del Capitaniato.

This, then, was the background against which a Vicentine architect worked in Venice. After his failure to obtain public office in 1554, Palladio submitted designs for the Rialto bridge and, the following year, for the Scala d'Oro in the Doge's Palace. A few years earlier, Michelangelo had submitted designs for the Rialto bridge, but Sansovino emerged as the clear favourite in 1555. For the Scala d'Oro, Palladio was in competition with five other architects, including Sansovino and Sanmicheli who entered a joint scheme that gained most support. The established success of both men in Venice was an obvious impediment to Palladio's career there. Although he had influential and active supporters in the Barbaros, it was Sansovino's patron, Vettor Grimani, who as the Procurator of St Mark's controlled the principal agency for public commissions in the city centre. Grimani and his fellow officer Antonio Cappello were two of the three commissioners appointed for the Rialto competition, so the final outcome can hardly have been a surprise.

Even though the route to a public commission in Venice was largely closed to Palladio, he persevered and made designs for several private works in the late 1550s. The first, in 1558, was for the façade of the Cathedral of S. Pietro di Castello, for the Patriarch of Venice. The contract named the Barbaro brothers as guarantors, but with the

60

death of the Patriarch in the following year the project quickly foundered. It was completed forty years later, after Palladio's own death, to a design which is Palladian in general effect but differs from that of the 1558 contract, which, for example, has 'six large columns' and 'six square pilasters, that is, three per side', as opposed to the four large columns flanked by two pairs of pilasters as built.

The façade of S. Pietro di Castello was Palladio's first major ecclesiastical commission. It was followed in the same year by the drum and cupola of Vicenza Cathedral. Helped by Daniele Barbaro, the brother who had most influence in the Venetian Church, Palladio acquired several other commissions for religious groups. His next invitation was for a refectory and service quarters for the monastery of S. Giorgio Maggiore. Then came the Convent of the Carità, begun in 1560, which was as we have seen the project that most closely followed his interpretation of the House of the Ancients in the Barbaro *Vitruvius*. The *all'antica* approach was particularly appropriate in this instance since the Lateran Canons had strong associations with Rome, and would have been familiar with the proposition presented to them by Palladio as a development of the earlier Palazzo Farnese prototype. The Venetians must have found the Carità design shockingly severe compared to the more flamboyant highly ornamented 'Roman' architecture of Sansovino, to which they had become accustomed over the last thirty years or so. It was something of an ideological coup, then, for Palladio to receive the commission for the façade of a church designed by Sansovino, S. Francesco della Vigna, whilst the Carità was still only in the early stages of construction.

The commission for S. Francesco della Vigna had come to Sansovino through Doge Andrea Gritti, and a design and model were made in 1534. These were analysed in a report by Francesco Giorgi (a Franciscan attached to the church), which had Serlio and Titian amongst the signatories. This now famous report sets out the harmony and proportion that they considered the building should follow in significant detail, which Sansovino's design lacked. Sansovino duly amended the proportions and building proceeded, only to cease some time after the death of Gritti when the main body of the church had been completed. The Grimani family then took over responsibility, having purchased the right in 1542 to build the façade as a memorial to Doge Antonio Grimani. When work commenced on this in the early 1560s the patron was the Patriarch of Aquileia, Giovanni Grimani, a brother of Vettor, Sansovino's patron (who had died in 1558). There had been no love lost between the brothers, and since Daniele Barbaro was already set to succeed Giovanni on his death as Patriarch-Elect, and the Barbaros had a family chapel in the new church, it is likely that Giovanni Grimani readily agreed to take on Palladio as the architect.

Palladio largely ignored Sansovino's first design for the façade (which is known from a commemorative medal, dated 1534; later changes are unrecorded), as well as Francesco Giorgi's memorandum, which demanded that the façade 'should be in the form of a square, corresponding to the inside of the building, and from it one should be able to grasp the form of the building and all its proportions'. The friar had proposed the Doric order for the interior 'as being proper to the Saint to whom the church is dedicated and to the brethren who have to officiate in it'. While Doric is indeed used inside, Palladio chose the Corinthian order for the façade. It would appear his concern was to make the exterior more emblematic of the triumphant Grimani family than of the austere sanctity of St Francis.

The essentials of his design had been worked out for S. Pietro di Castello, though instead of the 'six square pilasters and six large columns', here there are two pilasters and four small and four large half-columns. As the construction of S. Pietro di Castello was delayed, the façade of S. Francesco della Vigna was the first physical manifestation of Palladio's revolutionary thoughts for the appearance of the contemporary church, ideas that very possibly were worked out in collaboration with Daniele Barbaro.

The principal motif of Palladio's church façades was the pedimented portico, the element he had described as having evolved from the primitive dwelling house. What symbolized shelter for the 'house of man' was, to his way of thinking, the ideal emblem of the new church – the 'house of God'. In the same way that Palladio was responding in his architecture to perceived natural hierarchies (of use, form, materials and arrangement), the Council of Trent asserted the 'natural' hierarchy of the Church over society. The Church was concerned to emphasize the pastoral role of its priests, in an attempt to reconcile the faith of the individual with the superior authority of the Church as God's only legitimate mediator: this was the substance of the Counter Reformation. Daniele Barbaro attended the Council at Trent, and Palladio accompanied him there at least once. It is reasonable to assume, then, that Palladio knew something of the thrust of Counter Reformation ideas. Indeed, the formal language of his church designs seems to respond to the Church's new directives.

38,47   Consider the interlocking double pediments of his façade designs.

38   Palladio: façade of S. Francesco della Vigna, Venice, 1562–70.

Together they may be taken as a visual conflation of the 'house of
man' and the 'house of God': the lower pediment spans the breadth
of the church occupied by man and his memorials, while the other,
more 'heavenly' pediment appears to thrust upwards on tall elegant
columns. Did Palladio intend this combination of motifs to be read as
a symbol of the reconciliation between man and the supreme
authority of God which the Council of Trent also sought to achieve?

There were antique precedents for the double pediment motif.
39   Palladio had shown it in his restoration of the Temple of Peace (the
name by which the Basilica of Maxentius was erroneously known
during the Renaissance): here, the lower and crowning pediments are
on the same wall plane, and the lower horizontal cornice is continuous. (There is, in addition, a low colonnade projecting out from the
façade, which is absent from Palladio's church designs.) Vitruvius had
described his own Basilica at Fano as having 'a double arrangement of
gables' (V, 1), and so it had been interpreted by Cesare Cesariano in his
40,162   *Vitruvius* of 1521. Even the venerated Pantheon had two pediments, as
Palladio shows in his *Quattro libri* (IV, 20), though they are not on the
same plane. These were potent sources, yet Palladio's Renaissance
predecessors had not managed to reconcile the cross-section of the

39   Palladio:
reconstruction of the
Temple of Peace/Basilica
of Maxentius, from the
Quattro libri, Book IV.
Above is a longitudinal
section of the portico and
two of the three groin
vaults; below, half-
elevation of the façade
and half cross-section.

40 The Pantheon, Rome. One pediment is on the portico, the other on the wall above and behind it. This 19th-century photograph shows that second pediment before restoration, but it also shows the now-removed 'ass's ears', the twin bell-towers added in the mid-1620s, recalling Palladio's Tempietto at Maser (Ill. 52).

traditional Christian church, in which a high central nave is flanked by lower side aisles or chapels, with a truly *all'antica* temple front. In comparison Palladio's church façades are convincing. This is because, to my mind, he successfully combined the authority of antiquity with the new forward-looking ambitions of the Catholic Church, a resolution of substance and spirit which brought about a quality of timelessness: no wonder his façades set the model for Venetian churches over the next two centuries.

Palladio's first opportunity to design an entire church came through the Benedictine monastery of S. Giorgio Maggiore, where he had recently completed the refectory and service quarters. Rebuilding of the monastery had been considered for over forty years, possibly prompted by the rebuilding of its sister house in Padua, S. Giustina, drawings of which had been published and a model made in Venice in the early 1520s. As the monastery contributed annually to Venice's celebration of St Stephen's Day (26 December) when the church was visited by the Doge, and is prominently situated across the water from the Doge's Palace, there was some pressure to maintain its prestige which was being threatened by the important rebuilding programmes of other Venetian orders – not least that of the Franciscan Observants attached to S. Francesco della Vigna.

In 1564 the new abbot, Andrea Pampuro da Asolo, set about fulfilling his commitment to rebuild and appointed Palladio to produce a model, presumably as an extension of the work he had

65

completed satisfactorily on the refectory for the abbot's predecessor. The model Palladio made was, inevitably, a blend of his own ideas on the antique temple form, worked out in his two previous church façades, and the demands of the Benedictine Order. Renaissance humanists, following Vitruvius, had advocated two temple forms: the 'round' (which meant the centralized varieties – circular, polygonal, square, Greek cross, etc.), and the 'quadrangular' (based on the basilica) – the 'most beautiful, and most regular forms' as Palladio described them (IV, 2). The ancients fronted both types with a portico (Alberti, VII, 3). In Rome, the largely intact Pantheon was the most perfect exemplar of the 'round' temple, and the ruined Basilica of Maxentius/Temple of Peace was its 'quadrangular' counterpart. The latter consisted of a vast three-bay groin-vaulted nave buttressed on either side by enormous barrel vaults, of which three on one side survived. These two 'temples', the Pantheon and the Temple of Peace, were used frequently during the Renaissance as models for churches, and, as Palladio was aware, in the hands of Bramante and his successors they appear individually, and in combined forms (a quadrangular nave terminated by a rotunda), as alternative plans for the new St Peter's in Rome.

The Benedictines were clear about their needs and the form their church should take. When building S. Giustina in Padua, the Venetian branch of the Order had settled on a triple arrangement of a nave and flanking aisles. Palladio apparently followed this model for the plan of S. Giorgio, though he deviates from it in the section since his church has only one cupola, placed over the crossing, compared to the many that adorn the roof-line of S. Giustina. The transept arms are closed by semicircular apses, and at the head of the church lies a rectangular presbytery which is divided by a screen from the monks' choir.

The main body of the church, excluding the choir, bears some resemblance to Cosimo Bartoli's interpretative illustration of the *Templum Etruscum* or 'Etruscan Temple' in the edition of Alberti's architectural treatise that he had published in Florence in 1550. Bartoli had arrived in Venice in 1562; he remained there for the next decade as an agent for Florence, and his house was a meeting place for men like Palladio. In plan, his reconstruction of the 'Etruscan Temple' is cruciform: it consists of a rectangular main space with four central piers, off which three small spaces open (the largest at the end); in front is a tetrastyle portico. This is either a misreading or a loose interpretation of Alberti's description of a rectangular building having a central nave flanked on either side by three chapels, for

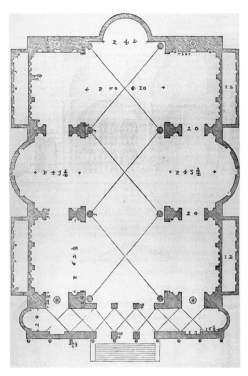

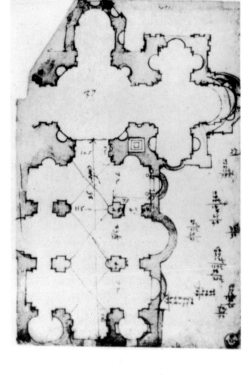

41 Palladio: plan of the Temple of Peace/Basilica of Maxentius, from the *Quattro libri*, Book IV.

42 *above right* Peruzzi: sketch plan for St Peter's, Rome, early 16th century.

43 *below* Bartoli: plan of the *Templum Etruscum*, from *L'architettura (De re aedificatoria) di Leon Battista Alberti*, 1550.

44 *right* Palladio: plan of S. Giorgio Maggiore, Venice, 1564–80. From Bertotti Scamozzi, *Fabbriche*, 1776–83.

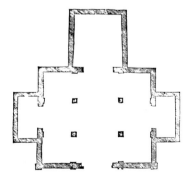

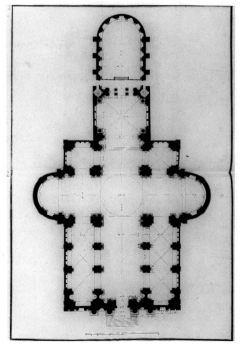

45 Serlio: reconstruction
of the longitudinal section
of the Temple of Peace/
Basilica of Maxentius,
from Book III, 1540/1619.

46, 47 *opposite* Palladio:
S. Giorgio Maggiore,
Venice, 1564–80, façade
1607–11. Longitudinal
section (from Bertotti
Scamozzi) and façade.

41 which the model was probably the Basilica of Maxentius/Temple of
45 Peace. Serlio's restoration of the Basilica/Temple (III, p. 59) shows
round-headed clerestory windows in the vault. Palladio adopts a
46 similar arrangement at S. Giorgio, though his are thermal windows at
high and low level, derived no doubt from his own studies of Roman
bath buildings.

It would appear, then, that Palladio's design for S. Giorgio
Maggiore is an interpretation of those principal ancient and modern
classical buildings whose forms were appropriate to the liturgical
requirements of the Benedictines: that is, the antique Basilica of
Maxentius restored by Serlio and himself, mediated perhaps through
the new St Peter's. Moreover, the Latin-cross plan, which the basilica
nave and rotunda crossing combine to describe, was important to
Palladio beyond any specific demands by his patron: 'because that
being fashioned in the form of the cross, [such plans] represent to the
eyes of the beholders that wood from which depended our salvation'
(IV, 2).

47 The façade of S. Giorgio further develops the experiment started at
38 S. Francesco, of a high portico of half-columns supporting a pediment
'overlapping' a lower portico. However, as it was not built until
1607–11, doubts have been raised whether it accurately follows
Palladio's intentions. An early preference was for a tetrastyle
freestanding portico comparable to that in Bartoli's 'Etruscan

68

Temple' illustration, a preference that he reasserted in four other church commissions, though it was adopted only once (at the Tempietto at Maser, described below). The portico, he argued, when describing the temples of the ancients, was necessary to provide shelter from the elements (IV, 5); but it was probably this very convenience that made it undesirable. As an influential critic of the portico Palladio later proposed for the front of S. Petronio in Bologna was to point out, 'the portico should not be built in any form whatsoever, lest it provide a receptacle for idlers and refuse'.

The façade that was built at S. Giorgio has an attached tetrastyle portico with half-columns raised high on pedestals, which, as at S. Francesco, is a distinct departure from the more common antique portico resting directly on the ground: similar half-columns and pedestals are used internally, so that the façade reads as an outward extension of the internal arrangement. The front of the pre-Palladian church was set inconspicuously well back from the water's edge, whereas the new one was intended to be clearly visible from a considerable distance: in that setting, a conventional portico might have appeared to be floating. The pedestals establish a positive foundation for the giant half-columns, which from across the water give the illusion of being fully rounded and freestanding, an effect enhanced by the swags apparently 'hanging' between their capitals (a motif perhaps influenced by those in Raphael's Chigi Chapel in Rome) and by the entablature that 'continues behind' them, supported by the lower pilasters that have their own independent rhythm.

Palladio had turned to the basilican type for his first church commission, because it most suited the liturgical needs of the Benedictines. His earliest ideas for his next church, the Redentore, were based on the 'round' model for reasons of symbolism, a circular plan being considered appropriate for a votive church.

The church of the Redentore – the Redeemer, the Saviour of mankind – commemorates some fifty thousand Venetian plague victims lost between the summers of 1575 and 1577. The vow to build it if the plague ceased was made by the Senate on 8 September 1576, the Feast Day of the Virgin's birth. In that same month two building commissioners were appointed, and by 22 November a decision had been made to build on the Giudecca in preference to an alternative site on the Grand Canal. Palladio, with Marc'Antonio Barbaro as his principal promoter (Daniele had died in 1570), presented a centralized design to the Venetian Senate. This was a square building, with a freestanding hexastyle portico in front and a semicircular apse at the east end. Inside, the square was transformed into a circle by the placing of paired columns in the corners, and this central space was surmounted by a dome.

Churches having a circular plan had been popular in northern Italy since the early twelfth century, soon after the Crusaders had liberated Jerusalem in 1099: they were modelled on the Church of the Holy Sepulchre – the first Christian *martyrium*, built by the Emperor Constantine, combining antique authority with Christianity. During the Quattrocento, 'round' buildings were associated with the Virgin (for reasons that Alberti listed: VII, 3, p. 195), or were used for martyrial, sepulchral and memorial buildings. There were liturgical problems, though, which were insurmountable, such as the position of the main altar within a centralized plan. Neither Palladio's drawings nor Marc'Antonio's oration to the Senate in favour of a 'rotunda' proved effective, and their bid was turned down in February 1577. The Senate asked for a 'quadrangular' design to be prepared, which would be more accommodating spatially. Within a week 'a design by our faithful Andrea Palladio in quadrangular form' was approved unanimously.

In fact, the design is more than 'quadrangular'. The nave is a well-defined rectangle with sides pierced by three arched openings which are framed by paired giant orders. But the area containing the altar is a centralized form – a square surmounted by a dome, and bounded by three enormous exedrae of Roman bath proportions. Two of these are curved walls (to the north and south), whilst that which separates the altar from the choir is a screen of four columns. Described in this way, the Redentore is a centralized memorial church with a congregational nave attached. There were Christian structures in Rome having a circular mausoleum attached to a longitudinal hall, which Palladio would have known (such as the Constantinian mausoleum of SS. Marcellino and Pietro, the so-called Tor Pignattara); or there was Alberti's Tempio Malatestiano in Rimini, which was planned originally to have a nave terminated by a rotunda, a connection of forms finally realized by Michelozzo and Alberti with the tribune of the SS. Annunziata in Florence. Palladio's design is more integrated than these earlier examples and is more akin to the various 16th-century proposals for rebuilding St Peter's in Rome, which combined the essential forms of the Basilica of Maxentius and the Pantheon in a Latin-cross plan. The Redentore is a compromise between symbolic intentions and the need to house a large congregation once a year, including the Doge and his full Council.

48–50

42

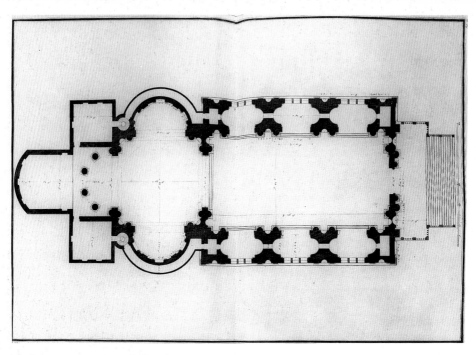

48–50   Palladio: the Redentore, Venice, *c.* 1576–80. Plan and longitudinal section
(from Bertotti Scamozzi), and interior, looking from the nave towards the altar
and the semi-circular screen of columns in front of the choir.

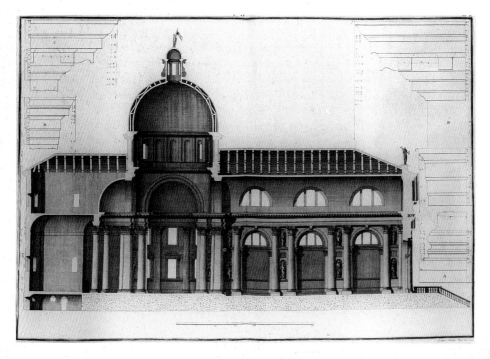

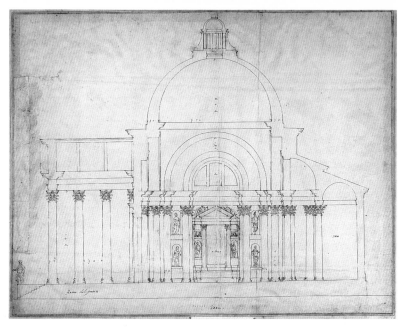

51 Palladio: design for a votive church (possibly the Redentore), longitudinal section.

52 Palladio: Tempietto Barbaro, Maser, c. 1580. The portico faces in the direction of the Villa Barbaro.

Palladio reconciled these aims within the narrow confines of the site with a building form which may have been influenced in particular by Giacomo Barozzi da Vignola's Gesù in Rome of 1568. Both churches may be compared formally and constructionally with Alberti's earlier S. Andrea in Mantua. Constructionally, for example, the naves of all three buildings have not continuous aisles but a sequence of chapels divided by fin walls that support barrel vaults over the chapels, which in turn buttress the high barrel vault over the nave (a form of construction evident too in the ruins of the Basilica of Maxentius, though there the lateral barrel vaults buttressed groins). Programmatically there were similarities. The Mantuans wanted 'a large space where many people could see the Blood of Christ' (a revered relic which was displayed only on Ascension day each year). Beyond the nave, however, the architects diverge in their symbolic intent. There is no direct source for the domed chamber that Palladio evolved for the Redentore except the constructionally and spatially impressive, but secular, bath buildings he had examined in Rome.

When Palladio had an opportunity to design a freestanding centralized *tempietto* in the late 1570s, unencumbered by liturgical or mass congregational demands, it turned out to be a much simpler, perhaps purer, architectural statement than his first designs for the Redentore. The Tempietto at Maser for Marc'Antonio Barbaro was   52 perhaps the realization of their original joint ambition for the Redentore, in miniature. The site, close to the Villa Barbaro, was not constrained by bordering buildings as its Venetian counterpart had been, so there was room to break out of the pure geometry of the circle and square, by superimposing a Greek-cross outline to provide three chapels of equal size. The interior has an exquisite spatial tautness, a product of its small scale and rich ornamentation. This ornamentation extends to the portico, the intercolumnation of which is garlanded as at S. Giorgio, but here in fully three-dimensional   47 form. The tympanum of the pediment depicts the martyrdom of St Paul, one of the patron saints of the adjacent community. The Tempietto has a stepped shallow dome like the Pantheon; and the   40 towers flanking the pediment prefigure the 'ass's ears' that were subsequently added to the Pantheon itself in the mid-1620s.

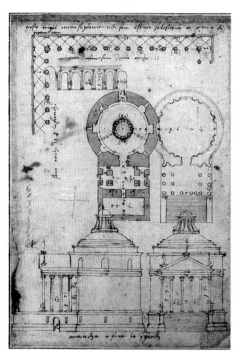

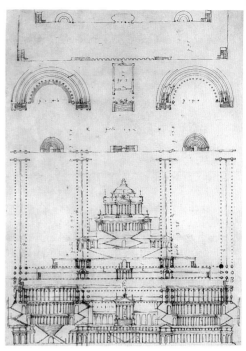

53 Palladio: reconstruction in plan and elevation of the Mausoleum of Romulus, late 1560s.

54 Palladio: reconstruction of the terraces and Temple of Fortuna Primigenia at Palestrina.

55 Palladio: reconstruction of the Roman theatre at Verona, showing it in elevation and part section, surmounted by a temple structure.

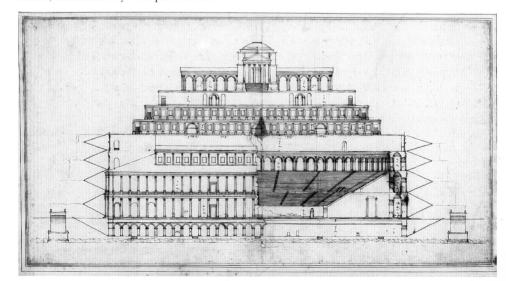

In a sense Palladio had been considering the design for the Tempietto   52
at Maser for some forty years, ever since the time when he copied some
drawings of Roman mausolea from Serlio's Book III. He included on
that sheet Serlio's plan of the so-called Mausoleum of Romulus, on
the Via Appia, which he accompanied with a fanciful reconstruction
of its elevation. This first exercise culminated in the late 1560s in a far
more convincing reconstruction of the Mausoleum of Romulus,   53
which has many of the characteristics of his eventual Tempietto
design: the raised platform, the hexastyle portico (which is three
columns deep like that proposed in the first Redentore design, and
reminiscent of the portico of the Pantheon), and the stepped saucer   40
dome, topped by a heavily buttressed lantern. The similarity between
the Tempietto and this antique mausoleum was entirely appropriate,
since it is likely that Marc'Antonio had the Tempietto built as a family
mausoleum, receiving a right of burial for the owners of the villa from
the papacy, in perpetuity, in 1585.

Another version of this Roman mausoleum design appeared in a
reconstructed elevation and part section of the Roman theatre at
Verona. Palladio had been fascinated by this structure since at least the   55
early 1540s, but the reconstruction with the Tempietto prototype has
been dated after that time. Only the lantern provided for the
Mausoleum of Romulus is missing. The model appears again in one
of his reconstructions of the Temple of Fortuna Primigenia at
Palestrina, the ancient Praeneste. Palladio made several reconstructions of the terraced sanctuary of Palestrina, with varying centralized
temples: one is like the Tempietto at Maser, one like the circular
colonnaded Temple of Vesta, while another has four porticoes around
a cylindrical core. The date of these drawings is uncertain. They may   54
have been made when Palladio's development of the villa was tending
towards a centralized temple-like form. The most famous of that type
is his suburban Villa Almerico, better known as the Rotonda (begun   56,61
1565/66), which is itself a development of the Villa Trissino at   62
Meledo, started nearly a decade before, around 1556–57.

What is common to the two villa projects and his fanciful
reconstructions is that the temple form is in an elevated position on
top of a hill. As Palladio writes of the Villa Trissino, 'The situation is
very beautiful, because it is upon a hill, . . . in the middle of a very
spacious plain. . . . Upon the summit of the hill, there is to be a round

hall, encompassed by rooms' (II, 15). Similarly, the Villa Rotonda is
56 built on a site which 'is as pleasant and as delightful as can be found;
because it is upon a small hill' with the river Bacchiglione on one side
and hills encompassing the other 'which look like a very great theatre'
(II, 3). Presumably Palladio was thinking of the theatre at Verona,
which stands in a city encompassed by hills and cut by a river (the
Adige), and, according to his earlier reconstruction, had at its top a
temple-like structure wrought by man's ingenuity and *virtù*.

62 At the Villa Trissino, the central house was to have been flanked by
great curving wings which focused the approach of visitors on a
principal entrance. The plan of the house itself has a biaxial symmetry,
to emphasize the primary and secondary roles of the porticoes, as
either entrances or viewing platforms. However, only some foundations and part of a wing were built.

The Villa Rotonda, which was mostly completed to Palladio's
design, was intended to be not a grand house but a suburban pleasure
house within easy reach of Vicenza, to be used for parties or
'recreation' as Palladio put it. Its proximity to an existing road meant
that a focusing device like a long axial drive was unnecessary (indeed,
the present drive and outbuilding are a later addition by Scamozzi). It
is as if Palladio wished the villa to appear isolated on its low hill, for
each hexastyle portico has equal emphasis, and the Rotonda is at one
with its natural theatre-like setting: at the centre of the changing
seasons, and the focus of man's cultivation of Nature.

Noble dwellings were usually defined as either urban or rural. The
palace enabled the owner to maintain a civic presence in the
proximity of rival nobles. The villa was a retreat from the pressures
and profanities of the city and, especially in the Veneto, was at the
centre of the family's wealth, which derived from land and
agricultural production. Dwellings which fell between these categor-
ies had been built in Rome: the Villa Giulia was close enough to the
Vatican for daytime visits only, as was Ligorio's pleasure house or
Casino ('small house') for Pope Pius IV in the Vatican Gardens. The
Rotonda belongs with that group. It was not the first design by
Palladio for a villa of this kind. He was in fact adapting for the
59 Rotonda his earlier design for the Villa Chiericati at Vancimuglio.

That villa was commissioned by Giovanni Chiericati, the brother
of Girolamo for whom Palladio had designed the Palazzo Chiericati.
Its design exhibits some significant 'firsts' for Palladio's architecture,
though its actual date is uncertain: suggestions have varied between
c. 1547/48 and 1554. It was the first of Palladio's villas not to be

78

surrounded by farm buildings, being designed simply as a country retreat from urban life. Depending on the date when it was designed,

64 it may have been the first to have a monumental portico-loggia on the entrance façade. Several of the details as built suggest that the design was an early experiment in Palladio's development of the ideal villa, but one which failed, for he excluded it from his *Quattro libri*. It is worthy of some attention here, however.

59 A plan of the Villa Chiericati, the only original drawing of the building to have survived, shows windows in close proximity to the

9 corners, as at the villas Godi and Zen – a practice Palladio was later to decry for reasons of potential structural instability (I, 25). The most likely precedent for this window and wall arrangement was the Odeo Cornaro, the music building to which Palladio had been introduced in his formative years in Padua, and which clearly fascinated Serlio

57 who published illustrations of it (though in the woodcut the plan

58 appears reversed) and made designs for villas inspired by it. The Odeo has two rectangular rooms at the front, entered from a central passage, with windows in one of the long walls flanking a central niche, the far window being close to the corner of the room, and so to the end of the façade. If rooms labelled G and F are erased from the Serlio plan, its relation to Palladio's drawing for the Villa Chiericati is reasonably close. However, closer still to the plan of the Odeo is that of the

61 Rotonda, which reads as a symmetrically perfected Odeo type with a version of the Chiericati façade attached to each of its four faces. One can only conjecture about the reasons for this correspondence: perhaps for Giovanni Chiericati, and the retired Monsignor Paolo Almerico, music was to be the principal source of 'recreation' in their exclusive villa-retreats.

The Odeo Cornaro appears to have been Palladio's inspiration for the first plans of the Villa Chiericati, but he moved away from it in the final building: the *sala* was cleared of stairs (which were moved to the adjacent spaces), and the apsidal ends with their niches, reminiscent of the Odeo's central octagonal *sala* and niches, were also deleted, to create a larger, almost square, space.

A suitable stair location had proven a problem for the plans of both the Odeo and the Villa Chiericati. In the Odeo the stairs take up room space and disturb the overall symmetry. At the Villa Chiericati there was evidently some disquiet as to their best position, though they are consistently kept to the rear. None of these locations was ideal for the centrally focused symbolical geometry of the Villa Rotonda. With its four main façades, the stairs could be concealed most effectively only

80

around the central core, where they would also offer additional support to the cupola. This move excluded the possibility of niches around the space, so from the octagonal form Palladio generated a more 'perfect' symbolism: of a circular plan inscribed within a square. The circle was the Pythagorean symbol of unified perfection, infinity and deity: indeed, it symbolized virtue to the early Christians. The square, conversely, was equated with the physical universe and the material world. Attempts at 'squaring the circle', from the Pythagoreans onward, reflect the desire to reduce infinity to something finite, or to transmute the divine to the physical realm. What could be more appropriate for the Villa Rotonda, which with its perfect natural setting, outward symmetry and temple-like appearance comes closer than any other to Palladio's ideal for the villa?

A house built by the painter Mantegna for himself in Mantua, dating from the late 1470s, is nearly square in plan and has an open central rotunda, surrounded by rooms. Its arrangement may have been suggested by contemporary experiments for centralized houses by the architect-engineer Francesco di Giorgio. Alternatively, Mantegna's inspiration may have been Alberti himself, whose church of S. Sebastiano lies diametrically opposite, and who held that ancient Roman houses usually had circular halls (IX, 3, p. 296). Mantegna's rotunda may or may not have been roofed (and either was acceptable to Alberti), but the general layout of the house, before it was extended at a later date, would have been of interest to Palladio. Even the size of the central rotundas is similar: Palladio indicated a diameter of 30 Vicentine feet, and Mantegna's is about $31\frac{1}{2}$ Vicentine feet (23.57 Mantuan *braccia* or 11m). The significance of this dimension is uncertain, yet clearly a cross-fertilization of ideas was taking place.

There are deviations from the Odeo design which are worth relating as they seem to derive from the ideal temple model that Palladio was developing, and show something of his thought process and method. The idea that the Villa Chiericati should have a full-scale portico is common to the surviving drawn plan and the building. The outer columns, which are shown engaged with the end walls of the portico in the plan, were built freestanding. The Ionic capitals of these outer columns are unusual, for the outer corner volutes are not parallel but angled: Palladio took this feature from the corner capitals of the Temple of Fortuna Virilis in Rome (which also has a tetrastyle portico), commenting later that he had not seen it anywhere else but thought it 'beautiful and graceful' (IV, 13). Similar corner volutes appear at the Basilica and in the upper central bay of the Palazzo

60

64

63

22

81

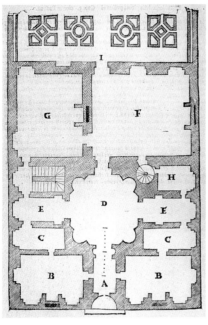

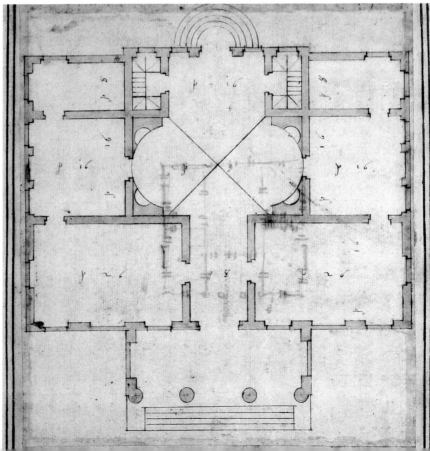

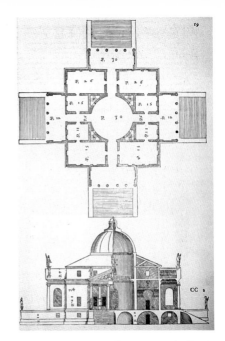

Opposite:

57 Serlio: (reversed) plan of the Odeo Cornaro, from Book VII, 1575/1619.

58 Serlio: design for a villa based on the Odeo Cornaro, from Book VII, 1575/84.

59 Palladio: plan project for the Villa Chiericati, Vancimuglio, *c.* 1548?

On this page:

60 Mantegna: plan of the artist's own house in Mantua, begun 1476 (shown to scale with the Villa Rotonda).

61 Palladio: plan and part elevation/section of the Villa Rotonda, begun 1565/66, from the *Quattro libri*, Book II.

62 Palladio: plan and elevation of the Villa Trissino, Meledo, begun *c.* 1556–57, from the *Quattro libri*, Book II.

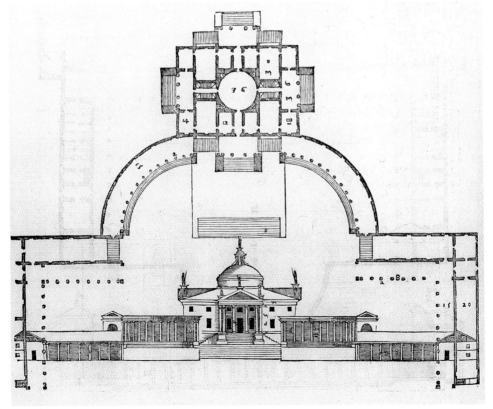

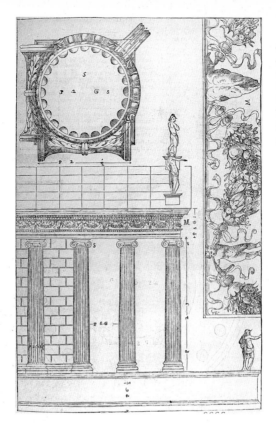

63 Palladio: part
elevation and details of
the Temple of Fortuna
Virilis, Rome, from the
Quattro libri, Book IV.
The Ionic capital shown
in plan at the top has an
angled corner volute.

25 Chiericati, which may suggest that the design of the Villa Chiericati
was contemporary with these buildings.

The walls with arched openings that terminate the portico of the
65 villa, a motif derived from the Portico of Octavia in Rome, also
terminate the porticoes of the Palazzo Chiericati. In the Portico of
Octavia, these arched openings frame the pedestrian passage under the
portico, as they do at the Palazzo Chiericati, whereas at the villa they
frame views – an inspired departure from the original. The Villa
56 Rotonda has the same arched motif ending its four porticoes, though
these are six columns wide (like the Portico of Octavia), not four;
there Palladio also abandoned the angled corner volutes, though he
continued to use the Ionic order (the Portico of Octavia is
Corinthian).

Palladio does not consistently use any one motif in preference to the
others. The arched motif terminating the porticoes of these villas does

84

64 Palladio: Villa Chiericati,
Vancimuglio, begun *c.* 1548? The
vulnerable angled volutes of the
outer column capitals have partly
weathered away.

65 Palladio: reconstruction of the
elevation and plan of the Portico of
Octavia in Rome.

66   Palladio: river front of the Villa Foscari, Malcontenta, *c.* 1558?–60. Note the stairs at the side of the portico.

not appear in the *tempietto* forms in Palladio's reconstructions of the Verona theatre, the Mausoleum of Romulus or the temple at Palestrina, which have porticoes two or three columns deep (like the Pantheon and other ancient temples). At the Villa Foscari at Malcontenta, built in the late 1550s, the portico is two and a half columns deep, Ionic, and has corner capitals with the angled volute. The two-storey portico appears at the Villa Cornaro at Piombino Dese, Villa Pisani at Montagnana, and Palazzo Antonini at Udine, which date from the early 1550s and are very similar in their appearance, planning and locations. The Villa Cornaro, although called a villa, is located within the town, as too is the Palazzo Antonini, and the Villa Pisani is just outside the city walls of Montagnana. The two-storey portico may have been influenced by an earlier palazzo-villa, the Villa Giustinian at Roncade, to the southeast of Treviso, close to Venice. This was built around 1500, by an unknown designer. The portico has two tiers of Tuscan columns supporting arches and a crowning pediment. As with this early villa, the portico of the Villa Cornaro protrudes from the entrance façade and there is an additional portico on the garden side recessed to align

86

67 Palladio: garden front of the Villa Cornaro, Piombino Dese, 1551–53.

68 Palladio: garden front of the Villa Pisani, Montagnana, c. 1552–55.

with the wall plane. The porticoes of the Palazzo Antonini and the Villa Pisani are recessed into the façades. In his subsequent villas Palladio adopts either approach without a clear preference for one or the other.

There are other villas by Palladio that do not have the single-storey temple-like portico. The early Villa Caldogno and Villa Poiana are practically unadorned, and their entrances are marked more simply: Caldogno has a triple arch motif, Poiana a serliana topped by oculi, probably derived from Bramante's Nymphaeum at Genazzano. Like the Villa Valmarana at Vigardolo, they are delightful in their simplicity. But with time, Palladio developed his villa and church architecture towards a perfection of emblem and form.

The ideal forms were centralized – though depending on location, site, and the functioning of the building, there were acceptable variations derived from the quadrangular, as antique precedent and Vitruvius suggested. In the villa, the implicit sacredness of the 'house' meant that profane areas connected with its workings (kitchens, stables, servants' quarters, etc.) were to be isolated as 'dependencies' of the main house. This expressive hierarchy was possible only with open sites, found usually in a rural setting. In cities, where space was scarce and expensive, Palladio had to restrict the outward expression of a palace to the confines of the façade. Within a dense urban context and especially with an irregular site, palace architecture can begin to reflect geometrical perfection only through captured space – the arrangement of indoor and outdoor rooms. Here, again, rooms tend towards the square and circle (be they the vestibule with its four columns supporting the *sala* above, courtyards, or ancillary spaces), though in overall form Palladio's palaces are quadrangular.

69   Palladio: entrance front of the Villa Poiana, Poiana Maggiore, *c.* 1549–60. The wall plane is modelled by slightly setting forward the central bay, and the entrance is emphasized by a flight of steps leading directly to the serliana.

During the first phase of Palladio's development, between 1540 and 1560, he had begun over thirty buildings, in and around Vicenza, of which about two-thirds were villas and the remainder palaces. All of the palaces of this early period have façades articulated as two separate storeys: either a rusticated base surmounted at the *piano nobile* by pilasters (often of the Composite order), as at the Palazzo Thiene; or, as at the Basilica and Palazzo Chiericati, a lower Doric order with Ionic above. Yet within this scheme definite changes are evident which parallel his development of the villa portico and possibly his early thoughts about the church façade.

17
22,25

The roots of change can be seen in the Palazzo da Porto Festa of the late 1540s. The façade as built is traditional enough, deriving from Bramante's 'House of Raphael' and the Palazzo Thiene. Indeed, there was a Thiene connection, as Giuseppe Porto who commissioned the work married Livia, the sister of Marc'Antonio Thiene, at about this time. A surviving drawing shows a façade composition in two storeys, much as built: a rusticated base supporting Ionic pilasters (with a pulvinated frieze), which are in turn surmounted by a low attic storey, designed as a support for statues, with pedestals separated by windows. The novel part of this design is the courtyard, which was to have had a Composite giant order standing directly on the ground and rising through two storeys. Placed between the columns at *piano nobile* level is a balcony; above them there is a bold cornice and a balustrade with statues. A very similar arrangement is found in the 'House of the Ancients' in the Barbaro *Vitruvius*, which was yet to be published.

10

70

32

Changes were occurring in Palladio's life at this time and he was responding to new influences. His mentor, Gian Giorgio Trissino, died in 1550. He was forging a new relationship with the Barbaro brothers at Maser, and the Barbaro *Vitruvius* was in preparation. Inevitably, through their own powerful contacts, the focus of his attention shifted away from Vicenza towards Venice. It is only after his early ecclesiastical work in Venice that the idea of the giant colonnade reasserted itself, on the façades of two Vicentine palaces of the 1560s: Palazzo Valmarana Braga and the Loggia del Capitaniato.

Palladio had begun to make improvements to the palace that Gian Alvise Valmarana had inherited after 1554, but this early work was superseded by a new design for Gian Alvise's widow made at the end of 1565, and commemorated in a foundation medal of the following

70   Palladio: project for the Palazzo da Porto Festa, Vicenza, late 1540s,

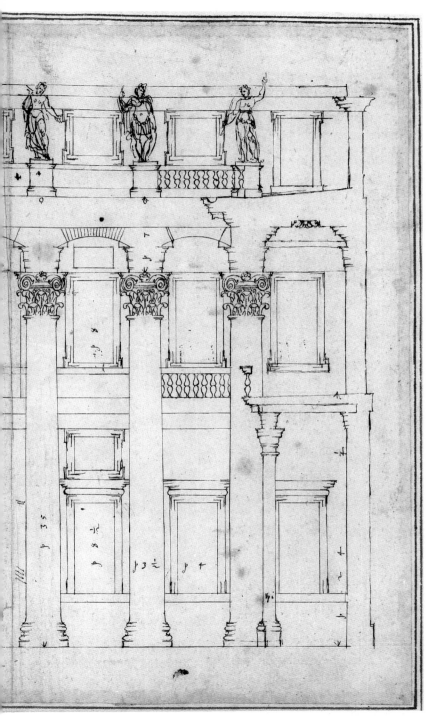

showing a half-elevation of the façade and half-section through the courtyard.

year. The site was not as symmetrical as Palladio presented it in the *Quattro libri*, though the basic layout, of a central axis punctuated by internal loggias separated by a simple courtyard, is the same. The façade belies this simplicity, with its classical motifs overlaying one another in a sophisticated illusionistic composition. Six giant Composite pilasters resting on a high plinth support a cornice and high attic storey; between them, balustered balconies are inset on the upper floor. The arrangement as a whole strongly recalls the court-yard elevation of the Palazzo da Porto Festa design. In addition, on the lower floor the bays are framed by a subsidiary order, this time Corinthian; and that order itself encloses a zone marked by rustication and divided into two tiers by a stringcourse. The effect is to synthesize the earlier two-storeyed façade type with the new giant order, and, through the use of various overlays, to create a quality of apparent depth and monumentality. A precedent for the giant order was provided by Michelangelo's east end of St Peter's in Rome: an even closer parallel to Palladio's scheme, with a subsidiary order, occurs in Michelangelo's Capitoline palaces, but these had been begun only two or three years earlier, and it is uncertain whether Palladio had seen drawings for them.

71 Palladio: Palazzo Valmarana, Vicenza, 1565–71, viewed down the narrow Corso Fogazzaro.

At each end of the Palazzo Valmarana façade Palladio evidently felt it desirable to make a transition from his giant order to the humbler elevations of the neighbouring houses. In these end bays the rhythm of the infilling elements changes, and the subsidiary order (which in the centre is threaded inconspicuously through the giant pilasters) emerges into its own. Above it Palladio places not another minor order but full-height relief sculptures of figures in Roman armour, an eccentric solution that could not be imitated elsewhere. These two features – the illusory 'depth' and the stepping-down of the end bays – are brilliant responses to the extreme narrowness of the street, which ensures that the building is always seen obliquely, never frontally.

In the Capitoline palaces the giant order was associated with a centre of civic power, and its use for a nobleman's palace might not seem entirely fitting. It appears again, however, more boldly expressed as half-columns, in a building which certainly was intended to symbolize authority: the Loggia del Capitaniato, which Palladio 72 may have designed concurrently with the Palazzo Valmarana (the City Council acquired land, possibly for a longer Loggia than was built, in 1565), although the final design may just postdate the publication in 1570 of the *Quattro libri*, from which it is absent. The new residence of the Capitano was to be a symbol of the Venetian Republic's presence in Vicenza. The Loggia, from which public declarations were read, faces onto the main Piazza dei Signori, across from the Basilica. The Venetian Commander was there to 22 maintain law and order within the city, and to ensure the obedience (if not the loyalty) of Vicenza. The Pedemuro workshop had provided running repairs on the existing building; their involvement, com-bined with Palladio's status locally and in Venice, where he was beginning to make his mark through private ecclesiastical commis-sions (in the early 1570s the Republic referred to him as 'our faithful Andrea Palladio'), may have encouraged the State to choose him as their architect, even though he had failed to obtain any public commissions in Venice.

We have seen that a number of Palladio's friends and clients in Vicenza were opposed to Venetian hegemony; but it is doubtful that this appointment troubled his conscience. The role of the humanist architect was to exhibit the *virtù* of his patron, and to celebrate God, the family, and the city. As Alberti had written (in Book V), the patron may be a private citizen, a prince or a tyrant: it was not the duty of the architect to judge between them, but to respond to their needs. The architect's concern was with beauty, which had to be

nurtured through experience and learning. Beauty was reliant on the intentions and abilities of the architect, which must themselves mirror the intentions and achievements of God through Nature, and of man in society. Palladio dealt with the eternal qualities of architecture which determine the essential fabric of society, and not the changing affairs of men and politics.

If Palladio could remain to some extent impartial, the Venetians were very partial, as they were in need of a counterbalance to the new loggias of the Basilica opposite which asserted the authority of the Vicentine nobles. Capitano Giovanni Battista Bernardo commissioned a design from Palladio to extend and reface the existing palace with a new loggia and a grand *salone*, and work began, probably in the spring of 1571. Construction proceeded more swiftly than on the Basilica, so that within eighteen months the Loggia, as the building came to be known, was completed in its present form.

The façade of the Loggia is articulated by four giant Composite half-columns. Some scholars have argued that what we have is only part of a much larger project. Documents exist relating to the purchase of property adjoining the Capitano's residence by the City Council, who intended to erect a new civic building which Palladio was likely to have been invited to design. But nothing was started, and whether the two buildings were intended to merge their identities is just one of many possibilities.

What was built does give the appearance of being a complete entity (particularly when viewed obliquely, from the Campanile end of the main piazza), and public loggias were traditionally three bays wide: examples are to be found in most Italian cities, where they were used to shelter and lend authority to dignitaries administering civic justice, and pomp and grandeur for those officiating at celebrations. The arcade at ground-floor level relates outward towards the piazza, and from here public proclamations were made and auctions held. The grand *salone* above is an internal extension of the old palace, with access (until the early 19th century) being only from the rooms behind. The Loggia, while symbolic of Venice's contributory role in maintaining the civic life of Vicenza, was welcomed by the City Council, who declared: 'it will be of such beauty that it will adorn our piazza to the marvel of everyone.'

The only overt symbolism is provided by the triumphal arch motif and stucco reliefs on the side elevation. The triumph being celebrated is the victory of the Venetian Republic and the Holy League over the Turks at Lepanto on 7 October 1571, part way during the building's

95

72   Palladio: Loggia del Capitaniato, Vicenza, c. 1565/71–72.

construction. The Vicentines had contributed men and galleys to this great naval victory, and the stuccoes of trophies, along with the crests of the patron, Capitano Bernardo, and the city of Vicenza, appear to celebrate the united commitment of the two cities.

The Loggia del Capitaniato boldly bares its brick construction, as had Palladio's Convent of the Carità. This was unusual, particularly for a public building. Palladio's other brick buildings are coated with stucco to suggest stone construction, and use stone at low levels vulnerable to damp and damage (see for instance the Palazzo Valmarana). His major public buildings – the Basilica and the church façades – are in white Istrian stone. The reasons for the use of brick are plain enough. Stone needs to be quarried, rough cut, transported and shaped, before being carefully hoisted into position. It is a slow, cumbersome and expensive process. Brick on the other hand can be produced locally in kilns, and is easy to handle and pre-shape. In consequence it was usually regarded as less prestigious than stone. Palladio did not consider it an inferior material, though, as the ancients had used it extensively in their buildings: his only comment on its preferred use was that when building grandly, the ancients used larger sized bricks than for private smaller buildings (I, 3). In any case, he believed that 'buildings are esteemed more for their form than for their materials'. The Loggia del Capitaniato, with its huge half-columns in brick, was thus in his mind by no means inferior to the apparently more magnificent Basilica.

The most elaborate formal proposition Palladio made for a palace façade appears in his rejected design for the Doge's Palace in Venice. This would surely have been his most prestigious commission, for the Doge's Palace was the political and administrative centre of the entire Venetian Republic. Here the Doge resided surrounded by the authority of the State, its executive and legislature. The ruling councils assembled here too – the Maggior Consiglio, composed of all adult Venetian nobles, and the Council of Ten, the national security council. Within its enveloping walls, in large and small chambers, government offices, and law courts, the entire authority of the Republic was focused. The diverse activities are matched by the varied ornamentation and materials of the enclosing walls, built at different times in different styles. Physical calamities, usually fire, had enabled parts of the building to be modernized and harmonized with the whole. The palace's most public and united face was turned towards the water and the Piazzetta, the direction from which most visiting dignitaries approached.

71

38,47

73

On landing at the Piazzetta, visitors today are greeted with an architectural backdrop which has changed little over the last four hundred years. As one disembarks, on the left the low horizontal colonnaded façade of Sansovino's Library – 'perhaps the richest and most ornate building since the time of the ancients', as Palladio described it – is terminated by the tall plain brick Campanile. The end and other side of the Piazzetta are in a markedly different architectural vocabulary, reflecting the glory of Venice's connection with Byzantium. The great arches of St Mark's, which close the space ahead, are set off on the right by the massive wall in pink and white marble of the Doge's Palace, punctuated by Gothic windows and long open galleries. Few urban spaces of this size can boast such a wealth and variety of architectural expression. Yet the permanence of this scene was threatened by two fires in the 1570s.

The chambers of the Senate and Collegio, to the rear of the palace, were gutted in 1574, though the exterior walls were saved. Sansovino had died four years earlier, and Palladio – thanks to the constant support offered him by Marc'Antonio Barbaro and the impact of his own reputation – was one of several advisors invited to present ideas on the building's refurbishment. Then, in December 1577, a more disastrous fire in the great Sala del Maggior Consiglio caused the upper floors and roof towards the Piazzetta and the water to become a mass of flames; a strong wind carried sparks towards Sansovino's Library and Mint opposite, but the fire was contained, and surprisingly the walls of the Palace remained intact. Again Palladio's advice was sought, along with that of other architects and engineers, and here he saw his golden opportunity.

According to a chronicler of the events, of all the advice received

only Andrea Palladio the celebrated and famous architect concluded that the façade towards S. Giorgio [i.e. to the water] should be destroyed and demolished, and the whole building substantially renewed, and this opinion of his was fomented by Marc'Antonio Barbaro, Procurator of St Mark's, a most able and prominent orator, to such an extent that although it appeared very extravagant to the whole Senate, all the same arguing with all his ability he kept the proposal alive for many days.

Barbaro would have been able to make much of Palladio's experience at the Basilica in Vicenza, but the only drawing that survives of the proposal for the Doge's Palace has none of the simple boldness of the Basilica, or, for that matter, of the Palazzo Valmarana and the Loggia del Capitaniato. Instead, Palladio presented a scheme that owes more

73 Palladio: project for
the Doge's Palace, Venice,
1578. The highly
articulated wall is divided
horizontally into three tiers,
and the arch motif of the
ground floor arcade is
extended vertically on the
central axis. The
rectangular windows are
ornamented with an
alternating rhythm of
triangular and segmental
pediments.

74 Palladio: Palazzo
Barbarano, Vicenza, built
between 1570 and 1575,
though the design may date
from the early 1550s.
Horizontal divisions are
clearly defined by the
cornices. The *piano nobile*
has the most refined
ornamentation, while the
lower storey is rusticated.
Although smaller than the
Doge's Palace, this building
gives an impression of
Palladio's intentions for
that façade.

to the palace façade he had built for Montano Barbaran in Vicenza, the Palazzo Barbarano, which had been recently completed, in 1575. 74 This Vicentine palace appeared in the *Quattro libri* with giant half-columns, but during construction Palladio reverted to the composition of his earlier palaces, with a horizontal emphasis provided by two superimposed orders, Composite over Ionic.

Looking closely at Palladio's Doge's Palace drawing, it would 73 appear that his concern was to respond positively to Sansovino's Library, and it is likely that he intended rebuilding not only the façade 2 towards S. Giorgio but that which faced the Library too. His design departs from Sansovino's in a number of ways: it is one storey taller; it uses a superimposition of Ionic, Corinthian and Composite orders where the Library has the more usual Doric and Ionic; and where on the *piano nobile* Sansovino has a sequence of identical serliana-like arches Palladio has windows, with alternately triangular and segmental pediments. Yet a number of details indicate Palladio's awareness of his building's illustrious neighbour, and his wish to harmonize with it. The arcade at piazza level, for instance, is similar in design and also raised by a few steps; the *piano nobile* windows are flanked by columns; and, most telling of all, although his building is a full storey taller, in order not to overwhelm the Library, Palladio made an unusual move: he set the top floor back by about the thickness of a column, and crowned the resulting 'two-storey' composition with statues. This would have had the effect within the Piazzetta of balancing the apparent height of the two façades, while from a distance the Doge's Palace would have been dominant. To stress its functional superiority, he provides a ceremonial entrance marked by three superimposed triumphal arches under a pediment, the whole resplendent with ornament, including the winged lion of St Mark. The entrance at ground floor level is emphasized by projecting columns surmounted by statues, an arrangement known to Palladio from the Arch of Constantine in Rome. The overall effect would have been to offer more unity to the architecture of the Piazzetta, whilst maintaining the relative hierarchies of its buildings. But the Senate would have none of Palladio's design, and they followed the recommendation of their advisors 'that the Palace should be restored neither more nor less than it was before'.

An indication of the surface effect that Palladio intended for the Doge's Palace can be gleaned from two built works, executed by his successor Vincenzo Scamozzi. In 1581, a year after Palladio's death at the Villa Barbaro at Maser, Scamozzi was invited to design the Procuratie Nuove on the Piazza S. Marco itself.

This palace for the 'New Procuracies' (actually a row of houses for the Procurators of St Mark's dressed as a single palace) runs on from the end façade of Sansovino's Library next to the Campanile. The two lowest storeys continue Sansovino's open arcade and arcaded windows, but an extra floor was demanded to provide additional accommodation. For this, Scamozzi appears to have taken the middle band of colonnette-flanked windows from Palladio's Doge's Palace project, and applied reclining figures over the pediments to complement the wealth of Sansovino-derived ornament beneath. The building was extended along the southern edge of the piazza over the next eighty years in a less ornate manner. Although it is a comfortable synthesis of Sansovinian and Palladian ideas, what Scamozzi's design lacks is the apparent depth which the layering of

75 Scamozzi: Procuratie Nuove, 1581, seen across the Piazza S. Marco. The end of Sansovino's Library and the campanile are to the left (cf. Ill. 2).

ornament had achieved for Palladio in his earlier palace façades, and which is evident in the Doge's Palace project both through the stepping-back of the vertical surface and through the modelling which the entablature surmounted by statues would have provided. Scamozzi was able to realize this general schema on Palladio's behalf for the *scaenae frons* – the stage setting, literally the 'scene front' – at the Teatro Olimpico.

78

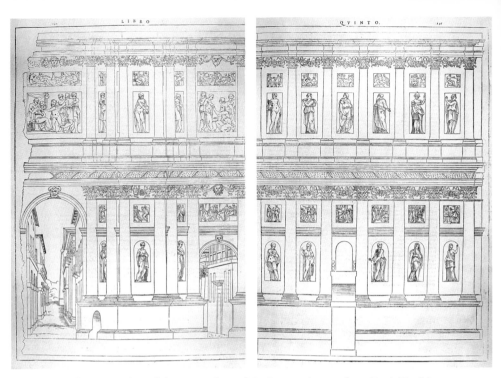

76   Reconstruction of the *scaenae frons* of the Roman theatre, from Book V of the
Barbaro *Vitruvius*, 1556.

77   Palladio: alternative 'scene fronts' and seating for the Teatro Olimpico, Vicenza,
1580 (drawn by his son, Marc' Antonio).

The Teatro Olimpico in Vicenza was the first permanent indoor theatre of the Renaissance. Whereas medieval mystery plays tended to be processional, urban spaces and buildings providing the backdrop, during the Quattrocento a specially contrived 'scene' became increasingly important. For private performances, the elaborate 'garden rooms' of villas were commonly used. The Villa Farnesina by Peruzzi had a theatre in its courtyard, and the Cornaro theatre has already been mentioned; but, unlike the permanent outdoor theatre Raphael had proposed for the Villa Madama, neither of these was intended to have permanent seating. Alternatively, palace courtyards were used, with performances being viewed from loggias. There were plays to suit either setting. According to the dictates of the classical theatre, tragedies required a sober urban backdrop, comedies a more vernacular and playful setting, and satyr plays a rustic or natural scene. Humanist preference was for the tragic, and Gian Giorgio Trissino had written the first Italian language tragedy, *Sophonisba*, in 1515, which popularized a form otherwise reserved for Latin scholars. The Barbaro *Vitruvius* contains a convincing reconstruction of the 'Roman Theatre', with its *scaenae frons* in imitation of a palace façade, as Vitruvius had described it.   76

Vicentine nobles had become familiar with current developments in the theatre ever since the Porto family had Serlio design a theatrical event for the courtyard of their palace, in 1539. Serlio records this temporary timber construction in a section in Book II, accompanied by a description of its semicircular auditorium. This, no doubt, owed something to Raphael's plan for the Villa Madama. Serlio also presented his ideas for the Tragic, Comic and Satyric scenes there, which he worked out for the Porto performance using all his skills as a painter. His stage had one large proscenium arch within which painted flats at the sides receded towards the back.

The effect was an unqualified success, and brought the Vicentine nobles much praise from their guests. Vicenza, declared one enthusiast, is 'more virtuous than Athens, greater than Milan, and richer than Venice, her mistress'. By consolidating itself as an independent centre of culture, the city enhanced its image abroad. The Accademia Olimpica was founded in 1555 to 'exalt those of its citizens who love *virtù*'. Within three years the first celebration of the 'ancient Olympic Games' was held, an academic spectacle expressing homage to Hercules, the Games' founder, for which Palladio provided certain constructions. These 'constructions' became more elaborate over the next few years, when the Academy promoted a comedy by Alessandro Piccolomini, *L'Amor costante*, followed by Trissino's tragedy, *Sophonisba*. These were performed in a semi-permanent wooden theatre in the *salone* of the Basilica, designed by Palladio to be dismantled and stored after use. Little is now known about its form, except that (interpreting commemorative frescoes of performances there) the stage probably had a triumphal arch proscenium, with one major and two minor openings framing streets either painted or constructed in perspective, and a semicircular auditorium.

When the learned Accademia Olimpica undertook to build a permanent theatre on a site granted to them by the City Council, in May 1580, it was to this triple-opening format that Palladio returned, though with modifications. The *cavea*, or auditorium, deviates from his preference for the semicircle because of site constraints, and is

77 elliptical in plan. His *scaenae frons* is more Vitruvian, in imitation of an
76 antique palace façade – in this instance, a blend of his Barbaro
73 *Vitruvius* reconstruction and his project for the Doge's Palace.

The idea already expressed at the Doge's Palace of a richly profiled lower level, with columns surmounted by statues flanking an arched opening, repeats itself here, although the articulation is more evenly distributed across the *scaenae frons*. The first floor colonnette-flanked windows reappear also, but in the form of aedicules filled with statues. All these statues had great significance for the Academy, and were intended to complement Palladio's design: 'each Academician should have his own statue made in stucco at his own expense with his name and motto and coat-of-arms engraved thereon, which statues must be placed on the column pedestals and in the niches in the aforementioned structure.' Panels at the attic level contain reliefs alluding to the Hercules myth, which is a reference to the founding of the Academy, as well as, more traditionally, the authority of the ruling class. Thus the proscenium, along with the classical arrangement of the whole theatre, was to become a permanent architectural and sculptural eulogy to the *virtù* of Palladio – who died in August, 1580 – and the noble Academicians. Even the changes that Palladio's successor Scamozzi made during its construction do not detract from this final testament to Palladio's career and the highly cultured environment that nurtured him.

By 1584 the building was nearing completion and thought was given to the first performance, for which Sophocles' *Oedipus Rex* had

104

been chosen. This tragedy required an appropriate urban setting, and Scamozzi was asked to design streets in perspective to represent ancient Thebes. Additional land had been purchased, after a petition in 1582, so that such streets could be constructed with the proper effect. The director of this play, Angelo Ingegneri, who had made his name in the court of Ferrara, was asked to consider aspects of the lighting and the design of the streets themselves, though this task fell ultimately to Scamozzi. The demands that Ingegneri made required Scamozzi to alter Palladio's design almost immediately. The openings which flank the higher central arch in the manner of the Arch of   78
Constantine were heightened to emphasize the 'streets' beyond, and the stage was narrowed by two new end walls with openings, between which a curtain could be hung. This is how the building was completed and so it has remained ever since, including the 'temporary' street scenes. On 3 March 1585, many of the audience arrived early with great anticipation. As the curtain rose, the distant sound of instruments and voices was heard echoing along the temple- and palace-lined streets, and the performance commenced.

78   Palladio and Scamozzi: interior of the Teatro Olimpico, Vicenza, 1580–85.

PART THREE

Palladio's architectural and literary legacy

I SCAMOZZI'S PALLADIAN INHERITANCE

The Teatro Olimpico was one of several projects inherited from Palladio by his most brilliant pupil and assistant, Vincenzo Scamozzi (1552–1616). Scamozzi's social and intellectual background was very different from Palladio's. He was a classically educated 'gentleman architect', not a mason who had to rise from the ranks. His father, Gian Domenico Scamozzi, was a successful surveyor and carpenter in Vicenza, credited by the humanist Lodovico Roncone with the independent design of three buildings, though in this he was probably only the collaborator of his son. It was Gian Domenico who kindled Vincenzo's enthusiasm for Serlio, and both of them contributed prefatory material to the first collected edition of his work, *Tutte l'opere d'architettura di S. Serlio* (1584).

Scamozzi's association with Palladio gave his career a vigorous start. While still in his early twenties, he designed the Palazzo Thiene-Bonin in Vicenza (after 1572), and completed the two bays which are all that was built of the Palazzo Porto Breganze, probably from a design by Palladio. When Palladio died Scamozzi inherited not only the Teatro Olimpico but also Palladio's principal patron in Venice, Marc'Antonio Barbaro, who obtained for him the commission for a great ducal tomb in the church of the Carità in 1582. In the same year 75 he was given the more important commission for the Procuratie Nuove.

In spite of these Palladian beginnings, Scamozzi gives the impression of wanting to distance himself from the old master. In his book *L'idea della architettura universale* (1615) he makes only occasional and oblique references to him, promoting instead a more intellectual approach to architecture and emphasizing its status as a Liberal Art. The differences between the two men can be summed up by contrasting the Teatro Olimpico with Scamozzi's Ducal Theatre at Sabbioneta and the Villa Rotonda with Scamozzi's Rocca Pisani.

The two theatres are very different spatially. Whereas the Teatro 78,79 Olimpico is wide and open, the Ducal Theatre is long and focused on

79 Scamozzi: Ducal Theatre, Sabbioneta, 1588–89, looking from the stage
towards the entrance, seating and rear colonnade.

the deep perspective of the stage. Instead of an almost semicircular
cavea based on ancient precedent, Scamozzi invented a horseshoe-
shaped seating arrangement which is entered through its centre.
Where Palladio was attempting to recreate a Roman theatre,
Scamozzi developed from that base in order to accommodate the
demands of the contemporary theatre, with a deep stage rather than a
shallow platform in front of a *scaenae frons*.

Scamozzi's answer to the Rotonda prototype is similarly responsive to use and need. He knew the Rotonda intimately, having completed its construction after Palladio's death. The lanternless saucer-shaped dome and the outbuildings by the entrance gate are both departures from the illustrations Palladio published of the building, and have been attributed to Scamozzi as critical interventions. Certainly, the villa he designed in 1576 for Vettor Pisani has a low dome without a lantern. The Rocca Pisani at Lonigo is actually derived from the plans of both the Rotonda and the Odeo Cornaro. After Palladio (or perhaps Serlio), Scamozzi designed a rotunda 30 Venetian feet wide placed within an overall square, and a hexastyle Ionic portico flanked by single windows. The four niches in the central rotunda, the off-centre stairs and bi-axial symmetry are closer to the details of the Odeo.

Both the Rotonda and the Rocca Pisani are pleasure retreats set on the top of low hills, with magnificent views over the surrounding

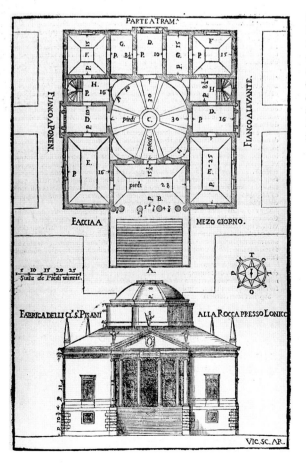

80, 81 Scamozzi: Rocca Pisani, Lonigo, 1576. Plan of the principal floor and southern elevation from *L'idea della architettura universale*, 1615, Book III, and view from the south-east.

countryside. Scamozzi, however, does not share Palladio's obsession with symmetry. Palladio's four equal porticoes symbolically relate the countryside to the central space, but he seems less concerned with making truly habitable rooms. Scamozzi has only one portico. On the other three sides the views are framed by open loggias in the form of serlianas which provide good light and breezes for the interiors lying behind them. Palladio's quest for purity based on the antique interpretation of Nature, a sort of archaeological classicism, is replaced by a willingness to adapt and respond to circumstances.

Scamozzi's work is generally seen in the context of that of Palladio, but he belongs much more to the mainstream, and might more usefully be compared with Sansovino. In his *Idea* he shows his intellectual capacity to theorize and to rationalize the architecture of the Renaissance as a complete body of work. Scamozzi was no maverick.

Palladio's completed buildings alone would have assured him a place in architectural history. His palace architecture, in its various forms, dominates the relatively compact city of Vicenza. His church architecture had made a significant impact on Venice, aided, in particular, by the highly visible presence of S. Giorgio Maggiore across the Lagoon from the Doge's Palace. But what ensured his reputation, and made Palladianism possible, was his decision to publish his architectural output and ideas.

We must assume that this was a calculated move and that he wished to be compared with the great architect-writers who had preceded him, especially Vitruvius and Alberti. His determination to write such a text may have been fired by Trissino's own brief attempt at writing the definitive architectural treatise, begun because of his dissatisfaction with the available texts on classicism:

> for having read Vitruvius attentively . . . I find that those things which at his time were very familiar are now entirely unknown . . . and that this Vitruvius is very badly understood and that he teaches nobody sufficiently in that art. . . . Leon Battista Alberti wanted to follow in his footsteps . . . but apart from the length of his treatise, it appears to me that one misses in it many things while one finds many which are superfluous.

The Barbaro *Vitruvius* was an opportunity, through Barbaro's commentary and the accompanying illustrations, to make the classical message clear. But Palladio seems not to have been satisfied with this, and even before it was published in 1556, his own manuscript was under way. From the evidence of *I quattro libri dell'architettura*, published in 1570, he was after something less wordy and erudite than either Alberti or Barbaro, and making more use of the illustrations themselves.

For this publication, as in his architectural theory and practice, Palladio took his cue from Serlio. Serlio had demonstrated how persuasive images could be when accompanied by brief descriptions and a short introduction. He had shown, too, through his own designs that the distant message of Vitruvius could be applied to any number of current situations, and for the benefit of society. More personally, the project had obviously benefited Serlio's own career, the publication of Books IV and III being swiftly followed by an invitation to enter the service of François I of France. Indeed, was Palladio's decision to assemble his four books for publication in 1570 prompted opportunistically by the withdrawal from active practice of Sansovino, who was by then close to death? He did seem to be in something of a hurry, although the publication had been in preparation for over fifteen years: in Book II, chapter 3, he relates the changes he had recently made to the design of the Palazzo Barbarano, though the woodcut was left unrevised since there was 'insufficient time' to have it recut.

Just as much of Palladio's architecture is a refined and focused version of Serlio's designs, so the *Quattro libri* are a refinement of Serlio's publications. Palladio's text is economical and to the point and buildings are described through illustrations, usually in plan, section and elevation, often on a single sheet. In addition, the dimensions of the buildings and their respective parts appear on the woodcuts, thus avoiding the lengthy recounting of dimensions in the text which readers of Serlio have to suffer. Palladio's text concentrates on three aspects of specific buildings: the patron, the site, and the use. Points of interest are noted and rooms are described. The images, on the other hand, show how the buildings were contrived – their size, configuration, and ornamentation. Underlying this, and occasionally interspersed with it, is an account of the principles of classical architecture. By dealing with classicism in a direct and accessible way, omitting much of the theory that makes up the treatises of Vitruvius, Alberti and Serlio, Palladio produced the first truly popular treatise on architecture.

Book I begins with the preparations for building: foundations and materials; the design and detail of the five orders, the choice of which determines the proportions of the whole building (he includes here a shorthand method for determining the entasis of columns – or as he calls it, to avoid unfamiliar Greek jargon, the 'swellings'); the types of rooms, their proportion, flooring and covering (vaults, etc.); doors, windows, stairs and chimneys; and finally roofs. Book II moves on to characterize the private house, first the palace and then the villa: he reconstructs the Greek and Roman palace, and goes on to show how to adapt ancient forms to modern requirements, listing most of his own palace and villa designs, including some unbuilt projects. Book III is concerned with public spaces, roads, bridges, and the ancient basilica, which, again, are illustrated by his own projects. Book IV is devoted mainly to the ancient temples of Rome. As Serlio had done before him, Palladio includes in this section examples of the work in Rome of Bramante – 'the first who brought good and beautiful architecture to light'.

All the buildings are presented in orthogonal form, as true plans, sections and elevations. Unlike Serlio, Palladio rejected the use of perspective: perspective drawings may please the eye, but it is difficult to take precise dimensions off them. The problem with an orthogonal elevation is that all the relief appears reduced to one plane: to remedy this, Palladio used shading to indicate projection and recession.

The *Quattro libri* thus had a twofold advantage: the text presented the true principles of 'natural' architecture in a concise form; and the illustrations were clear and precise, and conveyed the information needed for them to be imitated or interpreted according to need. By the 16th century printed books had become a powerful medium for the dissemination of ideas: the Reformation, for instance, could never have happened as it did without their wide circulation. Palladio established an international reputation after his death through having brilliantly exploited the same medium to disseminate his own interpretation of the classical method.

The future of Palladianism was thus not bound to the Italian peninsula, though there was an important Palladian revival in Venice which began in the early 18th century, prompted by a reaction to the 'extravagant' style of the Late Baroque. The earliest neo-Palladians there were Domenico Rossi and Andrea Tirali. Tommaso Temanza was to become the movement's most learned and able proponent, providing an intellectual basis which the initial revival lacked, but he was something of a pedant, and what had initially been a relatively free interpretation of the visual heritage of Palladio became increasingly codified by 'more correct' rules and theories, and drifted, perhaps inevitably, to Neoclassicism. But not before exerting a powerful influence on art and architecture in England, where there was similar resistance to the excesses of the Baroque.

Venice was then a major stopping-off point for the English Grand Tourists. A market developed for souvenirs – drawings, paintings and sculpture – which was coordinated for some time in Venice by the English Consul Joseph Smith, who acted as a dealer, impresario and publisher. Smith patronized the view-painter Canaletto, one of several Venetian artists, including Sebastiano and Marco Ricci and Giovanni Antonio Pellegrini, who visited England and were taken up by English nobles who were enthusiastic supporters of their brand of Italian art. This was because 18th-century England had a Palladian heritage in its own right, which it too was reviving at this time. Indeed, there was a direct line of contact between Palladio, Scamozzi and the great English Palladian Inigo Jones.

82 Palladio: reconstruction of the Temple of the Sun and Moon/Venus and Roma, Rome, from the *Quattro libri*, Book IV. This is a page from Inigo Jones's copy of the 1601 edition, with his annotations in the margin. He is concerned to analyse the proportions of the design and its refinements. 'Noat that the Statues on the Acroterri', he writes, 'are much bigger then thos ouer ye collomes being farder from the eye & to agree with the bignes of the collom.' He observes that 'this facciata is of Palladios inuention' and resembles that of the Temple of Peace (Ill. 39), and that 'the lodgs before and ornaments wthin ar added by Palladio as he immagenes the[y] had bynn'. The portico influenced Jones's design for the front of St Paul's, London (Ill. 100).

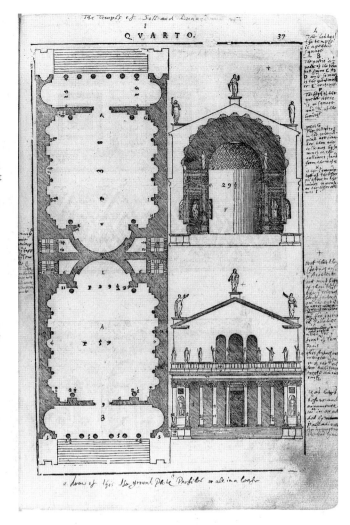

In the summer of 1614, Inigo Jones arrived in Vicenza. While he was there, armed with his copy of Palladio's *Quattro libri*, which he annotated copiously, he met the aged Vincenzo Scamozzi. Jones found the notoriously irascible architect secretive and 'purblind', but he was able to obtain original drawings by Palladio and so do what Scamozzi had no intention of doing, carry forth the banner of Vitruvio-Palladianism.

82

83 Portrait of Inigo Jones in his sixties by Anthony van Dyck, *c.* 1640
(a drawing once owned by Lord Burlington).

PART FOUR

Inigo Jones and the Stuart Court

I ENGLISH CLASSICISM AND JAMES I

That England was the first nation outside Italy to embrace a Vitruvio-Palladian architecture was due to the ambitions of the Stuart court as much as to the talent and activities of Inigo Jones.

Elizabethans had dabbled in Italian architectural theory and form, but there was never a decisive move towards a unified theory of architecture, and certainly no unity of theory and practice based on Vitruvian or Italian Renaissance experience. Italian treatises were read, but rarely in the original or in complete editions, as they arrived in England via the Flemish lowlands, where modified partial translations into English were printed. Direct experience of Italian architecture was unlikely: John Shute's *The First and Chief Groundes of Architecture*, of 1563, is the only English treatise based on first-hand study during this era. Shute had been sent to Italy thirteen years before by the Duke of Northumberland, 'ther to confer wt the doinges of ye skilful masters in architecture'. Whilst perhaps edifying for his noble patron, Shute's treatise appears to have had a negligible impact on current opinion. The Elizabethan court was not a forum for architectural debate, and Queen Elizabeth placed the onus of building on her courtiers' purses rather than the state's. The direction that architecture took was dependent largely on the idiosyncrasies of individual aristocrats, the architectural books they owned or could borrow, and the application of their builders, who were products of the masonic lodge system of training with its traditions rooted in medieval building practices.

The forms and underlying principles of classical architecture were known to the aristocratic patrons, and masons relied on their direction. Exactly how much they knew about architecture is shown by the private libraries which had been built up. By the early 17th century, for example, Sir Thomas Tresham in Northamptonshire, the Willoughbys of Wollaton outside Nottingham, and the 6th Earl of Northumberland owned copies of treatises by Alberti, Serlio, Palladio, Vignola, and the French architect-theorist Philibert Delorme, and what they lacked they borrowed from one another. This core of theory was important, but for classicism to succeed in England a wider dissemination of classical architectural theory and practice was necessary.

The 1611 English translation of Serlio's Books I–V, by Robert Peake, was an important contribution to 17th-century English architecture. It was at several removes from the original – being a translation of the Dutch edition of 1606, after the Flemish edition of 1553, which in turn was based on the Venice edition of 1551 – but the successful formula of clear illustrations and a complementary text was maintained, and it remained the best book in English on Italian architecture for about half a century.

An important interpretation of Italian classicism, for intellectual consumption, was written by Sir Henry Wotton, England's ambassador to Venice and a celebrated Italophile. His Vitruvian-inspired essay, called *The Elements of Architecture*, was published first in 1624, and ran to seven reprints by the middle of the next century. Its success shows something of the eagerness to have an authoritative account of classicism in the English language.

The appetite for classicism had grown in the early years of the 17th century. James I's entry into London for his coronation in 1604 was itself a sign of things to come, for the triumphal arch through which he passed was conceived in a quasi-Vitruvian manner. Its ornament had the more familiar flourishes of Netherlandish architecture, but the two side entrances were surmounted by obelisks, and the central arch was framed by Tuscan columns – 'the principal pillar of those five upon which the *Noble Frame of Architecture* doth stand' wrote the playwright Ben Jonson, one of the directors of ceremonies. The intention that lay behind this and other 'devices' was 'to present alwaies some one entire bodie, or figure, consisting of distinct members, and each of those expressing it selfe . . . with that generall harmonie so connexed, and disposed, as no one little part can be missing to the illustration of the whole'. This was more than a superficial rendering of Vitruvian and Albertian theory on a unified approach to design. All the principal elements of the arch were bound together by harmonic ratios derived from the ancient Pythagorean-Platonic divisions of the musical scale. As far as is known, it was the first time this rigorous approach was used in England.

James's right to rule was to be underpinned by promoting the ancient authority of kingship. The success of the Reformation in England had demolished the authority of the Pope, but the vacuum

84 A triumphal arch
for the coronation of
James I, from Stephen
Harrison's *Arches of
Triumph in London*,
1604.

that was left was filled by other authorities: the notion of the Divine
Right of Kings, and the authority of Scripture. These were combined
under King James I. As he proclaimed himself, 'The state of monarchy
is the supremist thing on earth; for Kings are not only God's
lieutenants on earth, but even by God himself they are called gods.'
And he was fond of comparing himself with the biblical King
Solomon whose name had likewise been invoked by the great
humanist popes, Pius II and Julius II, to lend authority to their rule
over the Catholic Church.

117

The unification of the Scottish and English monarchies which James's coronation (as James VI of Scotland and I of England) brought about confirmed him in his role of wise lawgiver. His reputation for statesmanlike wisdom would have been crowned if he had been able to realize the even more ambitious scheme of reunifying Protestant and Catholic Europe. On the Protestant side, he successfully forged a marriage between his daughter Elizabeth and the Protestant Elector Palatine, Frederick V; but when he tried to marry his son Charles to the Catholic Infanta Maria of Spain he failed, as her father, Philip III, spoilingly demanded the Prince's conversion to Catholicism.

This flexing of regal authority took on a more symbolical form within the confines of the royal court, using the potent structure of the masque. Masques were a form of allegorical drama in which stories from classical mythology were adapted to convey contemporary meanings. Kings, queens and princes were represented – and sometimes actually appeared – in the guise of gods and goddesses, and the intrigue of power politics took on the poetry and universal significance of the court of heaven.

The devisers of the masques provided a narrative, specified allusions and ordered the spectacle. Performances were spoken, acted, danced and sung, and held together by elaborately contrived scenes. The most famous partnership of the Stuart court fused the literary skills of Ben Jonson and the vision and mechanical ingenuity of Inigo Jones. It was Jones's ability to characterize the Stuarts through images and emblems that brought him acknowledgment, fame and wealth, and led to his appointment as architect to the Crown. Indeed, by 1616, he was referred to glowingly by the poet George Chapman – himself the translator of Homer – as 'our only learned architect'. Jones's infiltration of the traditionally conservative domain of surveyors and master builders marks the beginning of a revolution in British architecture. Sir Christopher Wren's nephew recorded in the *Parentalia* (published in 1750), compiled in honour of his uncle, who was himself a prime exponent of the new professionalism:

Towards the end of King James I's Reign, and in the Beginning of his son's, Taste in Architecture made a bold step from Italy to England at once, and scarce staid a Moment to visit France by the Way. From the most profound Ignorance in Architecture . . . Inigo Jones started up, a Prodigy of Art, and vied even with his Master Palladio himself.

Jones's start in life, like that of his 'master' Palladio, was inauspicious enough. Information on it is equally sketchy. He was born in east London in 1573, and baptised 'Enego' there on 19 July. His father was probably Welsh, from Denbighshire, and a clothworker. In his mid-teens Inigo was apprenticed as a painter-joiner, a role in which he must have shown some promise, since by his mid-twenties he was in the service of the noble Manners family. In 1598 he set out on a tour that seems to have taken in France, Germany and Italy, probably with Francis Manners, Lord Roos, the brother of the Earl of Rutland, and he remained the family's 'picture-maker' for the next five years. He may have stayed in Italy until 1603, when in the summer he travelled with the Earl of Rutland's train to Denmark, where the Earl was to deliver the Order of the Garter to Christian IV on behalf of James I. Once there, he entered the service of King Christian, before returning to England the following year to work with Ben Jonson on masques for Christian's sister Anne of Denmark, the wife of King James.

Although the Danish connection marks the beginning of his successful career as a royal masque designer, his earlier trip to Italy provided him with an insight into Italian culture, untypical for an Englishman. The developments in Italian theatre would have been of particular interest for the masques he was now designing. With great vision, Edmund Bolton inscribed in a book on Sixtus V given to Jones in 1606 that through the latter's abilities, he hoped, 'sculpture, model-ling, architecture, painting, acting and all that is praiseworthy in the elegant arts of the ancients, may one day find their way across the Alps into our England'.

Jones made his first major architectural designs under the patronage of Sir Robert Cecil, Earl of Salisbury, for whom he had been designing entertainments since his return from the Continent in 1603. Cecil himself had been building since the turn of the century, first Salisbury House and then Hatfield House, in an exotic blend of Elizabethan, Flemish, Italian and French Renaissance styles. This was the manner promulgated by Simon Basil, Surveyor to the Crown, who was in control of the Office of Works.

Cecil may have been interested in promoting an alternative architecture to that of Simon Basil – or perhaps even an alternative architect. He certainly had the authority to do so on two projects in London: one for the New Exchange in the Strand, and the other for a replacement for the medieval crossing tower of St Paul's Cathedral. 85

85   Jones: elevation for the New Exchange in the Strand, London, 1608.

Cecil himself had acquired the Strand site for redevelopment, and he was a commissioner on behalf of James I for the cathedral tower project. They were two very major works for an unproven designer, and in the end Jones was no match for the established record of Simon Basil, whose design for the New Exchange was built, though no final decision was made on the tower.

At least Jones's aspirations and abilities as an architect had been brought to the attention of the Stuart Court, and perhaps this was what Cecil had planned. The designs Jones made are in any case transitional between the prevalent Jacobean style and the classicism *all'antica* that he was to embrace so convincingly. His New Exchange design contains the decorative elements of English architecture then current, particularly in the skyline with its tower-like lanterns, while the lower two storeys are more controlled and in an assertive classicism – including a central serliana, or, to call the motif by its English name, a Venetian window, that derives from Serlio's Book IV. There are similar traits in the cathedral tower design. The upper storey has three Venetian windows on each side – derived again from Serlio's Book IV, or perhaps from Jones's own experience of Palladio's Basilica, though the drawing style and the use of ornament are more obviously Serlian than Palladian.

85

120

The only design actually carried out that can be attributed to Inigo Jones without doubt at this time is the memorial to Lady Cotton at St Chad's, Norton-in-Hales, Shropshire. The date is uncertain: she died in 1606, and Jones's design of around 1610 was built and later amended to include Sir Rowland Cotton's effigy after his death in 1634. The first design bears all the hallmarks of Jones's current interests. The exaggerated false perspective created by the relationship of the foreground columns to those behind the sarcophagus reflects a painter's concern for apparent depth demanded by his theatrical designs from 1605 onwards. The sarcophagus appears in a scene from the *Barriers* for Sir Rowland Cotton's 'master', Prince Henry, held in 1610, and columns supporting globes (which are family arms in the built monument) appear in *Oberon*, performed twelve months later.

It was expected of Jones that his masque designs should have an emblematic content favourable to the Stuart Court, and it was inevitable that this should spill over into his architecture – that is, that architecture should convey meaning and reinforce the status of the patron, and his role in society. Classicism *all'antica* was an assertion of authority that reached back to the cradle of European civilization, and the birth of Christianity, and was identified with Italy, the current cultural centre of Europe. Classical architecture was therefore accepted as an essential touchstone of taste by those of the English Court intent on raising the nation's standing abroad. But, two hundred years after Italy's Renaissance, English art and architecture were still in many respects medieval. The development of Jonson and Jones's masques shows something of how attitudes were changing within the Stuart Court.

In their very first masque together, *The Masque of Blackness*, for Anne of Denmark, performed in 1604, Jones introduced scenic techniques unknown in England. Whereas the Elizabethan theatre had an open stage, Jones probably employed a proscenium arch here, as he did in his later masques. The performance began with a curtain painted with a hunt scene, which was dropped to reveal a seascape surmounted by a moon on an upper stage. The sea was made of moving waves interspersed with musicians disguised as tritons and mermaids. The ocean behind them was 'drawn by the lines of perspective, the whole work shooting downwards from the eye'.

Whilst by now perspective was commonplace in the Italian theatre, its use in this production was revolutionary, and largely lost on the provincial English: the Venetian ambassador considered it a 'very beautiful and sumptuous' performance, whereas more conservative factions described it as a 'pageant' with 'all fish and no water'. The allegory behind it was plain enough to understand. The Queen took part with her ladies, eleven of whom appeared as blackfaced nymphs of Niger; they accompanied her to Britannia, an island ruled by a Sun 'whose beams shine day and night', and their faces were bleached white. Such, the audience were shown, is the power of monarchy and of James I, the Sun-King.

Hymenaei (1606) was designed to celebrate the marriage of the children of the Earls of Essex and Suffolk, and Jonson used his writing skills to draw a parallel between this alliance and the 'marriage' of Scotland to England by James. Jones made allusions to a glorious antiquity in harmony with universal order. He set the stage with an altar at which a Roman marriage ceremony was taking place. Then, using a *machina versatilis* for the first time, the scene rotated on a pivot to reveal a spinning globe, out of which stepped eight lords representing humours and affections. From the upper stage where Juno was enthroned, clouds descended bearing ladies, his 'Powers'.

Over the next few years Cecil employed Jonson and Jones to provide spectacles in honour of the King and Queen, but in 1610 Jones had his best opportunity yet, when he was appointed Surveyor to Prince Henry, the heir to the throne. Henry gathered around him a formidable array of classically oriented artist-architects. He employed the French garden designer Salomon de Caus, who had already

worked on Queen Anne's gardens at Greenwich, and Constantino de' Servi, a Medicean architect from Florence, to design a great garden with fountains at Richmond. Henry brought Inigo Jones in for his advice too, and perhaps to coordinate their work and to mediate with the labourers. This garden was intended to rival any in Italy, with enormous sculptures: a 'great figure' was planned 'three times as large as the one at Pratolino'. Henry's predilections for Italian Renaissance culture were complimented by Robert Peake's dedication to the Prince of his 1611 English translation of Serlio. (Peake was also the Prince's 'picture maker'.) Whilst the masques by Jonson and Jones are sympathetic to this Italianizing spirit, it is framed within a Britannic myth which emphasizes the roots of English kingship and chivalry.

In the masque *The Barriers*, of 1610, Henry is portrayed as a Knight of the Round Table, the epitome of the English Age of Chivalry. The following year he is *Oberon, The Fairy Prince*, son of the legendary King Arthur, and he is dressed in the costume of a Roman Emperor. This performance introduced another innovation from Italy, the *scena ductilis*, where scenes are painted on shutters, which are withdrawn in succession. The scenes progress from natural rocky outcrops to the architecture of a castellated medieval palace bedecked with exotic classical ornamentation. The climax is a Golden Age, in which British chivalry and romance are combined with classical mythology and Roman order. 86,87

86, 87 Jones: designs for Oberon's Palace, for the masque *Oberon, The Fairy Prince*, 1610. The exterior of the palace (*opposite*), painted on shutters, would draw back to reveal a colonnaded rotunda within, and that scene would then revolve, by the use of a *machina versatilis*, to reveal the interior (*right*).

The tragic death of Prince Henry in November 1612, at the age of eighteen, deprived Britain of this particular vision of unity, and scattered the collective expertise which would have ensured its creation. In February 1613, however, his sister Elizabeth married Frederick V. Inigo Jones was part of the royal train that accompanied the newlyweds to Heidelberg, arriving there in June 1613. He had been chosen as the travelling companion of Thomas Howard, 2nd Earl of Arundel and Surrey, formerly a close supporter of Prince Henry, who led the entourage. The plan was to continue on south to Italy for a Grand Tour which was to last until January 1615. Jones was chosen as guide, 'by means of his language and experience in those parts'. He was then aged forty, compared to the Earl's twenty-eight, and was as much his instructor as his guide.

They reached Milan in July, and from there they moved eastward and took in Padua, Venice and Vicenza, before moving south-west via Bologna to Florence and Siena, arriving in Rome in November. There they stayed until the early summer of 1614, with periodic trips south to Naples. In July they returned to Venice and Vicenza, and there on 1 August 1614 Arundel and Jones encountered Vincenzo Scamozzi, then in his sixties and just two years from death. In September they set out for home, via Turin, Genoa and Paris, and reached England in January 1615.

They brought back with them paintings, sculptures and miniatures, books on art and architecture, and drawings. Jones had taken with him twenty books from his already established library, and these he annotated assiduously: his 1601 edition of the *Quattro libri* is littered with notes and direct observations. His enthusiasm was shared and encouraged by Arundel, who bought several chests of original drawings by Palladio and Scamozzi. Sir Henry Wotton, the English ambassador in Venice, owned some of Palladio's drawings and may have aided Arundel's purchase. Arundel kept for himself two chests, probably of Scamozzi's drawings, and passed on to Jones preliminary drawings by Palladio for private and public buildings, as well as drawings by Scamozzi.

Even if Scamozzi had been reluctant verbally to put his knowledge of Italian architecture at the Englishmen's disposal and was intent on a broader interpretation of classicism, Jones had by then had time to form his own opinions on Palladio and Scamozzi's practice of

architecture. The collection of drawings by Palladio that he acquired supplemented, and even surpassed, the woodcuts in the *Quattro libri*, and proved to be the catalyst and the sustainer of the movement that Jones had initiated in England. It was undoubtedly a constant source of information and inspiration as it passed from one promoter of its architectural message to another for more than a century, exhibiting the working of a design approach more fully than the final woodcuts, stripped of inconsistencies and doubts, could ever do. The year of Jones's return to England, 1615, may be counted as the beginning of English Palladianism, since in September that year Simon Basil died and Jones succeeded him, as the most cultured and well-informed Surveyor of the King's Works the English Crown had ever known. Prophetically, he staged the masque *The Golden Age Restored*, and a new era of classicism was initiated in England.

A fully formed classicism did not develop immediately. It took Jones time to assimilate the experience and knowledge gained on his last Italian trip. Also, he had to redirect the energies of the workforce he had taken over from Basil, and train them to meet his own new and more rigorous architectural standards.

In the year of his appointment as Surveyor, Jones began work on a house for Queen Anne on the site of an old gatehouse which straddled a public road between the palace and the park at Greenwich, downstream from the city of London. It can be surmised from surviving drawings that the design that was approved had two porticoes, facing north and south (towards palace and park, respectively), and that on the end elevations the road was bridged at first floor level with a depressed arch and a Venetian window above. The Queen died in 1619, and no further progress was made for over a decade. When James I died in 1625 his eldest surviving son, Charles, became king and the property was transferred to his queen, Henrietta Maria. As the earlier design had reached no higher than the rusticated base, revisions were possible and were undoubtedly made. The house was not completed until 1638, by which time Jones had made most of his finest designs. It is very much simpler and more refined than the first version, and indeed is the most cubic and pure of all his house designs. The Queen's House bears no direct resemblance to any one house by Palladio, which is a point worth emphasizing: Jones was concerned to revive the spirit of antiquity through architecture, and any resemblance in his buildings to Palladio's designs, which is rare, is a byproduct of their common admiration for the antique. Jones was no less original a classicist than Palladio himself.

Two important private commissions in the first years of his appointment came from his close relationship with Lord Arundel. He remodelled Arundel's house at Greenwich, though within two years a fire had destroyed all that had been done. And he designed a gallery at Arundel House in London for the Earl's recently acquired collection of antique sculpture. Daniel Mytens's portrait of the Earl includes in the background a view of this barrel-vaulted room, lit by openings in one wall and concluded by a railed balcony overlooking the Thames. Within the same period, c. 1615–19, Jones partially refaced and refenestrated the exterior in a general campaign of modernization. There was a fair amount of compromise in these and other commissions, since the aim was to update and improve existing properties. This must have proved frustrating for Jones now that potentially he was in such a powerful position to build anew.

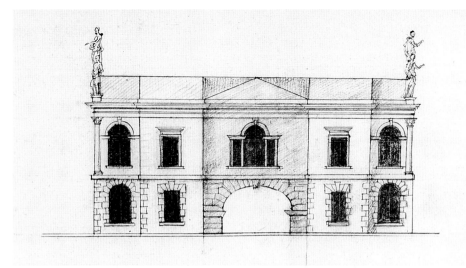

89   Jones: preliminary design for the side elevation of the Queen's House, Greenwich, 1616.

90   Jones: entrance front of the Queen's House, Greenwich, 1638.

91, 92   Webb after Jones: elevation and longitudinal section of the Star Chamber in the Palace of Westminster, 1617. (Webb's drawings, of the 1660s, introduced some modifications; the building is longer, for instance, and the pedimented centre projects further than in Jones's surviving plan.)

By the time of Jones's appointment as Surveyor State building was in fact in decline, and while he made a number of designs his opportunities to realize them proved to be limited.

The first of his designs which rigorously reflects the Vitruvio-Palladian tradition was that for the King's Star Chamber, dated 1617. The façade shown is seven bays wide, with the emphasis on the three central bays, where a giant fluted Corinthian order resting on a rusticated base supports a pediment; plain pilasters frame the ends of the composition. Only its rather diminutive, ill-proportioned windows suggest its early date. The idea of a dominant centrepiece with windowed bays on either side may have been influenced by Palladio's reconstruction of the House of the Ancients and culled from Jones's copies of the *Quattro libri* and the Barbaro *Vitruvius*. The internal arrangement reflects the building's proposed use as a prerogative court presided over by the King and his council, for which the plan of the ancient basilica 'where justice was administered' was eminently suitable. As Palladio explained, there were no surviving ancient basilicas in his own time, only descriptions by Vitruvius. The details Vitruvius gave of his own design for the Basilica at Fano are the basis of the reconstruction of the form in the Barbaro edition, which Palladio amended for the *Quattro libri*. Both plans are based on the double square – Vitruvius's 30 × 60 feet, Palladio's 60 × 120 feet. Palladio's design has colonnades on three sides, while for the fourth he proposed an apsed tribune. The Basilica at Fano has colonnades on all four sides, with a smaller number of bays, and the tribune projects externally from one of the long sides. Like Palladio's reconstruction, the Star Chamber is a double-height rectangular space concluded by a tribune, where the King would sit in judgment. Here the Stuart dynasty intended to rule supreme without the restraint of Parliament, ensuring their own economic wellbeing by levying taxes which Parliament would never have approved. In the end, although the Star Chamber functioned as a legal institution, Jones's design was never built. It was realized in another form, however, with the construction a few years later of the Banqueting House.

Several designs of around this time are based on the same characteristically Palladian formula of a projecting centre flanked by recessed bays that are treated more simply. The Prince's Lodging at

91

34

92

30

93 Newmarket, as designed in 1618–19, was to have been seven bays
wide, with the three central bays surmounted by a pediment. In one
scheme the projecting centre resembles Palladio's Villa Forni-
Fracanzan façade (not published in the *Quattro libri*), although there
are suggestions of Serlian influence too, in the dormers above the
cornice. As built, the Prince's Lodging was only five bays wide;
whether it had a pediment or not is impossible to determine, as it was
demolished less than forty years later.

The only design from this period with a pediment that was
definitely built is the Queen's Chapel at St James's Palace. Its
foundation stone was laid on 16 May 1623, and it was completed two
94 years later. The west front incorporates the central arched opening
and end quoins of the Newmarket design, and like it is devoid of any
orders. It is, in fact, a curious blend of a 'house' exterior and a 'temple'
95 interior. The coffered vault is based on Palladio's reconstruction of
82 what he called the Temple of the Sun and Moon (actually, the Temple
of Venus and Roma), in Book IV of the *Quattro libri*. Apart from the
ceiling Jones uses ornament sparingly. At the east end there is a large
Venetian window, the first time this motif was built in a design by
Jones. The chapel was intended for a Catholic Queen, but, ironically,
its unencumbered and austere rectangular space proved to be more
suited to the simple practices advocated by Protestants, which focused
on the preacher, than to the elaborate liturgy favoured by the Roman
Catholic Church.

130

93   *opposite* Jones: façade
elevation for the Prince's
Lodging at Newmarket,
1618–19.

94, 95   Jones: the Queen's
Chapel, St James's Palace,
London, 1623–25. View
from the northwest, and
engraving of the interior
looking east, showing the
chapel as fitted out in
1686–88 for the Catholic
Queen of James II.

The combination of a simple rectangular plan with a tripartite
96–98 elevation reappears at the Banqueting House in Whitehall, intended
for royal entertainments and masques, which was begun in 1619 and
completed in 1622. This has a rusticated base with small square
windows, and above that two superimposed orders, Ionic below and
Composite above. The three central bays are emphasized by half-
and three-quarter-columns, while the side bays have pilasters,
doubled at the ends. The columns, although applied to the wall surface, have entasis, and the Ionic frieze is pulvinate, both features char-
91   acteristic of Palladio's ornamentation. As in the designs for the Star
Chamber, with which the Banqueting House bears comparison, a central pediment appears in the early projects but was later abandoned.

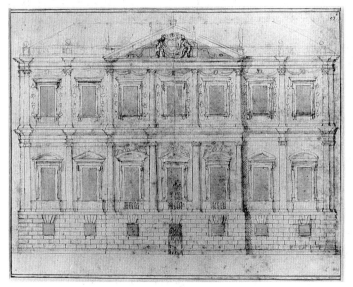

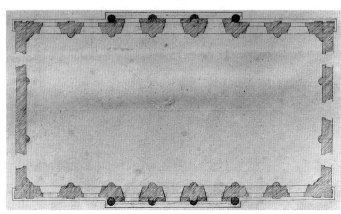

Jones: the Banqueting
House, Whitehall
Palace, London,
1619–22.

96   Elevation of the
penultimate design,
1619, with a pediment
and ornamented upper
floor windows.

97   Main floor plan as
executed, 1619, with
pronounced
centralizing features
front and rear, and
without the tribune
that appeared in earlier
designs. (Record
drawing by Webb
after Jones.)

98   *opposite* The
façade to Whitehall.
Later refacing in
Portland stone
destroyed Jones's
intended effect of
horizontal banding,
achieved with different
coloured stone, which
countered the vertical
push of the orders.

Early designs for the interior have walls divided by the orders into seven bays on the long sides and three at the ends, as in Vitruvius's Basilica at Fano, although the perimeter aisle is absent. Jones appears to be 'correcting' Palladio in this instance and following the Vitruvian exemplar more faithfully – though he too originally provided a semicircular tribune on the end wall. In the overall dimensions, however, he compromised. His building was the third structure on the site; its predecessor had measured 53 × 120 feet. Jones opted for a double square not of Palladio's more 'perfect' 60 × 120 feet but of 55 × 110 feet, with an internal height of 55 feet, making the space a double cube. He seems to have had a somewhat ambivalent regard for the mystical value of numbers.

There is evidence in his annotated copy of the *Quattro libri* that he made an attempt to come to terms with Palladio's use of number and measure. As he notes, rather convolutedly (the spelling has been regularized): 'The Vicentine is more than our English foot by 2 inches or one 6th part and the inch more than [an] inch by 6th part, all the designs in this book are measured by this foot.' Put more simply, the Vicentine foot is 14 English inches long; the ratio between them is 12:14, so that 6 Vicentine feet (V.ft) = 7 English feet. He begins the process of computation on the following page with the plan of the Palazzo Antonini, inscribing the equivalent English dimensions in a box adjacent to Palladio's number: thus 8, 17, 24, 28 and 32 V.ft become 9ft 4in., 19ft 10in., 28ft, 32ft 8in., and 37ft 4in. Not surprisingly, Jones did not carry on with this process of conversion, since only one dimension had produced an integer in English feet. When, occasionally, he did make a comparison, he used approximations: thus he rendered the width of a wooden bridge, 34½ V.ft, as 40ft instead of the precise equivalent, 40ft 3in.

It is true that the numbers (and forms) Palladio records in the *Quattro libri* are often idealized and deviate slightly from what was built. And it is possible, had Jones published his own designs, that their dimensions would have been regularised, for he attached great importance to the use of a repeating module throughout a design (a column or masonry block width), and his plans (and to some extent the elevations) are controlled by obvious geometrical figures such as the square and triangle, and principal rooms may be cubic – or double cubes, as with the Banqueting House. The Saloon of the Queen's House is a 40-foot cube, and ancillary room dimensions are subdivisible by 5 and 8 feet. Harmonic ratios order the room sizes, but generally Jones's designs lack the rigorous application of harmonic numbers found in the buildings of Alberti and the drawings of Palladio. Publicly, it would seem, Jones's concern for the correct use of numbers was not ambivalent – at least, that is, if we are to believe a passage in Ben Jonson's masque, *Love's Welcome to Bolsover*. There the architect, identified as 'Coronell Vitruvius', shouts to the carver, mason and joiner: 'Well done, my Musicall, Arithmeticall, Geometricall Gamesters! It is carried in number, weight, and measure as if the Aires were all in harmonie, and the figures in well-timed Proportion.'

At the Banqueting House Jones used a module derived from the column diameter of the orders, a practice perhaps encouraged by Scamozzi (who, in Book VII of the *Idea*, systematizes the five orders according to a module based on the column diameters). Even the size of the rusticated blocks is governed by the module. This careful controlling of elements was originally enlivened by the use of stone of varying shades: the rusticated base 16 feet high (a perfect number but one that appears in isolation) was of a honey-coloured Oxfordshire stone; the upper walls and orders were of a darker brown Northamptonshire stone; and the balustrades were of white and highly durable Portland stone. This subtle polychromy was lost as the darker and softer stone deteriorated, and the building was gradually refaced entirely in Portland stone (under the direction first of Sir William Chambers, and then of Sir John Soane).

99 Jones: interior of the Banqueting House, with its two superimposed orders separated by a balcony. The throne was at the far end of the space seen here. The magnificent Rubens ceiling (installed by 1635) expounds the virtues of kingship and the Divine Right to rule.

Internally, the most arresting feature is the brilliant ceiling by Peter 99
Paul Rubens, which glorifies James I as the new Solomon. The eventual installation of the panels, by 1635, meant the end of the Banqueting House's role as a masquing hall, as it was soon noticed that the smoke from these torchlit events was damaging the paintings. It remained the Court's principal ceremonial hall. Jones's architectural conception *all'antica*, and the programmatic content of the paintings by Rubens, was a potent combination which underlined the activities and vision of the Stuart Court. In the Banqueting House there was a new unity of architecture and painting, of theme and message, which was an exemplar for the future.

The large scale of the Banqueting House is quite startling when seen in the context of early 17th-century London, something which is forgotten now that it too is dwarfed. The combination of its size and of the requirement that it should have a flat ceiling led Jones to introduce Italian roof construction methods which were new to England. Traditionally roofs were arch-braced, and the hammer-beam 'truss' was used for the largest spans. But this system required heavy timber members, which was wasteful of material and

100 St Paul's, London, as remodelled by Jones in 1633–42. The visual effect was of a curious blend of Gothic and classical elements. Engraving by Wenceslaus Hollar from William Dugdale, *The History of St Paul's Cathedral*, 1658.

expensive, although it was admired for its technical achievement and so proudly displayed as an ornament. From his Italian travels, and from the literature of the Italian Renaissance – principally the Barbaro *Vitruvius*, Serlio and Palladio – Jones knew a structure that was lighter, since it used continuous horizontal ties (requiring only a small section) supporting a system of triangulated timber members above, which resulted in a lower pitch externally and provided a flat soffit internally. He directed his craftsmen to construct such a truss for the Banqueting House.

This constructional innovation was but one of many changes that Jones introduced in his attempt to achieve a rigorously classical type of building in England. Every project required his constant and detailed involvement: there were no built precedents in England to which Jones could refer his men. He had to re-educate his builders and masons, and to relay a constant flow of information, technical and theoretical.

The deliberate association of the Court of King James with classicism had more to it than mere stylistic preference. If the arts and society were imbued with universal harmony, then by implication the Stuart King was not only the nation's ruler but, more fundamentally, he was an influential force behind heavenly and

136

terrestrial order. The masques did much to project this image within the ambience of the Court, and in so doing reaffirmed allegiances amongst the aristocracy. But they were ephemeral; and Jones, through his mastery of the classical language of architecture, had the power to express the same message in the more permanent and visible form of major public buildings. The Banqueting House was the first realization of this, but there were more grandiose schemes to follow, of which the refacing of old St Paul's Cathedral was the only one to be carried out. 100

After his abortive work on St Paul's in 1608, Jones received the commission for a more extensive programme of modernization to the cathedral. Considerable sums of money had to be raised, and it was not until Charles succeeded James in 1625 and Laud became Bishop of London in 1628 that the future of Jones's designs seemed more certain. Still, it was 1633 before he received instructions to commence an impressive programme which in its most ambitious conception was to make London a 'new Jerusalem'. The medieval transepts and nave were dressed in a classical skin, and the west front completely remodelled. The foundations for the great portico were dug in 1635, paid for personally by the King.

The programme of restoration was completed in 1642, and the new portico surmounted by statues, including James and Charles amidst the Saxon kings, was a feat which could be compared with any of the achievements of the ancients or moderns: its height of 56 feet to the top of the entablature matched that of the Pantheon portico, and of the giant order of Michelangelo's Campidoglio in Rome.

Jones partly based his design for the west front of St Paul's on Palladio's reconstruction of the 'Temple of the Sun and Moon', which had been 'dedicated and built', Jones observed in his *Quattro libri*, 'by 82 T. Tatio King of the Romans'. How appropriate its form was, then, for the King of the Britons. It had an even deeper significance than this. As Jones continued, 'This *facciata* is of Palladio's invention and was used for the front of the Temple of Peace.' The importance of the 39 'Temple of Peace' or Basilica of Maxentius for the Renaissance and Palladio's church architecture has been already touched on. It was not only considered to be 'the greatest and most magnificent of the city', as Jones commented, but was believed to have been the repository of the plundered treasures of the Temple of Solomon in Jerusalem. The papacy had claimed that Rome was the legitimate successor of Jerusalem in the 15th and 16th centuries. The Stuart Kings were preparing London to rival that claim.

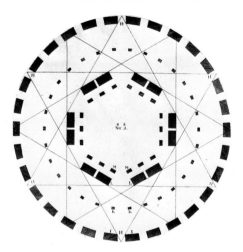

101 Jones: plan of Stonehenge, as regularized geometrically using four equilateral triangles inscribed within a circle. From John Webb, *Stone-Heng Restored*, 1655.

To sustain such a claim, a king of Britain had to do two things – rewrite history, and provide himself with a convincing architectural heritage. The result was what has been called the 'Britannic myth'. The 'myth' was that Britain had its own sound classical tradition. This had been obscured by the invasion of the Goths and by Gothic architecture, but with the right kind of dedication it could be revealed again. Jonson and Jones referred to this in *Oberon*:

> More truth of architecture there was blazed
> Than lived in all the ignorant Goths have razed.
> There porticos were built, and seats for knights
> That watched for all adventures, days and nights:
> The niches filled with statues to invite
> Young valours forth by their old forms to fight,
> With arcs triumphal for their actions done . . .

Jones was required by King James to investigate this heritage further during his Surveyorship, with a specific brief to explore Britain's most famous ancient monument, Stonehenge. The results of his study, although not published in his lifetime, aroused a controversy that lasted, with architectural repercussions, into the next century.

Having surveyed the stones, Jones reasoned that the underlying order and proportions of Stonehenge were such that it was certainly an ancient Roman temple, not one built by the Druids as had been held hitherto. Although relationships had been observed between the stones and heavenly bodies it was unreasonable, he argued, to assume this was the work of the Druids:

was not the Temple at Hierusalem adorned with the figures of Cherubims, that thereby the Nations of the Earth might know it was the habitation of the living God? and why not in like manner this Temple composed by Astrologicall figures, that after Ages might apprehend, it was anciently consecrated to Coelus?

Coelus, or Uranus, is the god of heaven, the oldest of the classical gods: according to Jones, this was the clue not only to Stonehenge's relationship with the heavens but to the archaic form of its Tuscan-like orders, the standing stones. Its circular plan, the most perfect temple form, he found to be governed by four equilateral triangles 101 rotated around the centre point, an arrangement described by Vitruvius (and drawn by Palladio) for determining the plans of Greek 31 and Roman theatres. The evidence for its consecration to Coelus was provided by Valeriano's encyclopaedia of symbolism, the *Hierogly-phica* of 1602, which Jones had used for the symbolic content of his masque designs: 'not only . . . the circular form, but the mere segment of the circle amongst the Egyptians was an hieroglyphic of Coelus', and the equilateral triangle is 'the figure whereby the ancients expressed what appertained to heaven and divine mysteries'.

   With these discoveries to hand, Jones could present the King with an argument highly supportive of his regime. Ancient Britain had its own classical, God-given architecture; this temple was in harmony with the stars and the universe; it was consecrated not to some minor deity but to God the Father; it displays the authority of ancient classicism in its form and severe, but wholly appropriate, ornamentation; the purity of its form reflects the purity of the Protestant faith, and as such is a fitting symbol for the new Britain and the monarch.

   James I died before the great symbol of his reign, the remodelled St Paul's, was realized; the Banqueting House was built, though the painted ceiling by Rubens, with its iconographic programme which hailed his authority as the unifier of England and Scotland, and as the British Solomon, was not in place until a decade after his death. The funeral oration by the Bishop of Norwich, entitled 'Great Britain's Salomon', made his achievements clear nonetheless: central to it was the message that a new era had begun, that King James was a modern monarch in whom antique virtue was reborn. It was now up to his son Charles I to translate his father's love of virtue into enduring symbols of the Stuart dynasty and of a revived Great Britain.

The most ambitious of James's proposals that Charles was to revitalize was the notion of a new palace on a Solomonic scale, a *Domicilium regni* to match the *Domicilium religionis*, St Paul's. It is possible that the Banqueting House had been conceived not in isolation but as the first part of a much larger new palace complex. However, the first hard evidence that Jones was designing such a palace comes from the late 1630s, well into the reign of Charles I.

Several schemes survive for a site in Whitehall, which would have obliterated the old palace and the Banqueting House, and for a site in nearby St James's. The so-called 'P' scheme for the St James's site consists of an assemblage of linear buildings arranged around a series of large colonnaded courtyards, some completely enclosed and some open on one side. The entrance court is circular. Beyond it is a huge square central space, with on axis on its far side the royal chapel, a centralized form with three equal arms. The whole enormous ensemble of courtyards and rooms was comparable in scale to Bramante's work at the Vatican, the proposals underway at the Louvre in Paris, and the Escorial in Spain, centres of power both real and symbolic with which the Stuarts wished to vie.

The model that Jones referred to for the palace designs was not directly Palladian. Palladio had admired and reconstructed the ancient

102

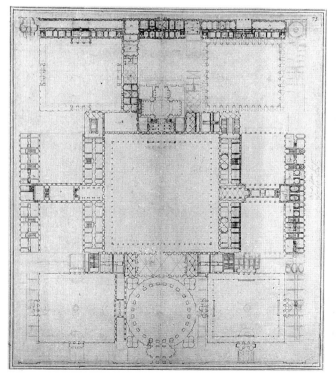

102   Webb, probably after Jones: plan project for a palace in St James's Park – 'P' or preliminary scheme, *c.* 1638.

Roman baths which were on a similar scale, but he had never conceived of building anything so large. Jones may indeed have learnt a good deal from the baths plans himself, but his direct model for the new palace was most probably the reconstruction of the Temple and Palace of King Solomon which the Spanish Jesuit Juan Bautista Villalpando made on the basis of Biblical accounts and subsequent commentaries, and published as an appendix to his *De Postrema Ezechielis Prophetae Visione* (1605). That work was in the library of James I, and it is possible that a Solomonic enterprise of the kind Jones was preparing had been considered by the Court for some time.

Villalpando had been educated in the court of Philip II, who was in many ways a model for James I – monarch of an empire, champion of Christianity, and wise lawgiver. Philip's domain extended from Naples and Milan in Italy to Spanish South America. His son, Philip III, was king by the time James succeeded to the English throne, and this great Catholic dynasty was an illustrious example to the Protestant Stuarts. Aware of the fortune Philip had amassed from South America, James had seized the initiative in North America, and his determination to build a new palace in London surely stemmed from the magnificence of the Escorial, outside Madrid, completed for Philip in the latter part of the 16th century.

103 Villalpando: reconstruction of the plan of King Solomon's Palace and Temple, from *De Postrema Ezechielis Prophetae Visione*, 1605.

104　Juan de Herrera: the Escorial, 1563–84. Bird's-eye view by Pierre Perret, 1587.

The palace-monastery of the Escorial reflected Philip's Solomonic pretensions in its form and enormous scale. It is not surprising that it inspired Villalpando's own reconstruction, especially as his instructor in mathematics had been Juan de Herrera, the architect of the Escorial. Jones was apparently aware of both models. Formally, his palace plan is closer to Villalpando's reconstruction than to the Escorial, though a principal elevation of a later design, in Webb's hand, is close to the Escorial. A broader intellectual tradition unites all these designs, however, which is a blend of Vitruvian and Christian thinking, a synthesis to which Villalpando made reference in his second volume. Villalpando concluded that Solomon's Temple was the ultimate source of the Greek and Roman orders which Vitruvius had described, and that the Palace should be upheld as the archetype of classical harmony in architecture. He believed the harmony God had disclosed to Solomon was the form of musical harmony which Pythagoras and Plato had 'discovered', and used that to rationalize the proportional system recounted by Vitruvius. In doing so he echoed Barbaro's own commentary on Vitruvius.

Although there is no textual evidence to prove Jones had read Villalpando, his interpretation of Stonehenge and the close correspondence between his drawings and the Escorial/Palace of Solomon give us an indication of his thorough understanding of classical principles and how they may be seen to accord with Christian beliefs.

142

While his most important projects were designed for the Court, Jones's message was extended beyond its circle. Perhaps his most original contribution to the tradition of Christianizing classical principles is to be found in his design for the church of St Paul's, Covent Garden, which was part of a development that also gave London its first formal urban space. In 1631 Francis, 4th Earl of 105 Bedford, set out to build a mixture of houses and shops just north of the Strand. His choice of Jones as his architect was no doubt influenced by the fact that Jones was the executive officer of a commission set up in 1618 to review London building practices. The design for Covent Garden reflected not only the principles adopted by the commission (avoidance of high density, sound construction in brick) but also new Continental experience, especially in Italy and France, in achieving a total civic environment. Jones's plan has a 'Grand Piazza' at its centre which is rectangular and bounded by 'houses and buildings fit for the habitations of Gentlemen and men of ability' to the north and east. Their ground floor incorporates an arcade reminiscent of the Place Royale (now the Place des Vosges) laid out by Henry IV in Paris, which Jones may have seen when he made a visit to Paris in 1609. But Jones's composition was on a smaller scale, and the south side was left as an open garden (which his own land adjoined). At the west end he positioned the church of St Paul, placed centrally and flanked by gates leading into the churchyard. This juxtaposition of a church and a formal open space recalls the late 16th-century arrangement at Leghorn in Italy, which John Evelyn (the English translator of Fréart de Chambray's *Parallèle de l'architecture*, in 1664) took to be Jones's model for Covent Garden. More fundamentally, of course, this 'temple–forum' arrangement is rooted in classical antiquity, and was revived in the Renaissance from Vitruvian theory.

St Paul's, Covent Garden, was built quickly, within a year. It was the first completely new church in London since the Reformation, and the first wholly classical church in England. In the interests of economy and in conformity with Bedford's Low Church preferences, Jones's brief was to produce a simple structure not 'much better than a barn'. Jones's dignified reply is said to have been that the Earl should have 'the handsomest barn in England'. As his model he took the Vitruvian 'Tuscan Temple', perhaps inspired by Giuseppe Viola Zanini's reconstruction of that temple type in *Della Architettura* 106 (1626), a copy of which Jones owned.

The simple interior, no more than a plain rectangular auditorium with a pulpit and altar, was ideal for preaching. The Tuscan portico is not in fact the entrance to the church (which is at the other end), and is unconnected with the interior: it performs a purely civic role in the 'piazza', where it was echoed by the arcades under the new dwellings. Both the arcades and the elevations of the habitations above are based on examples published by Serlio. The natural rusticity of Jones's composition, where a church portico is flanked by garden gates, is in marked contrast to the high sophistication of Venetian Catholicism, and set a tone highly sympathetic to the austerity of the Protestant cause. His association with that vision did not spare him from the indignities he was soon to suffer in the Civil War, when his allegiance to the Crown led to his imprisonment by men more vigorously puritanical than he.

The Civil War, which broke out in 1642 and consumed most of the last decade of Jones's life, put paid to any further major building opportunities. As 'the King's Surveyor, and Contriver of Scenes for

105 *above* Jones: Covent Garden, London, 1631–34. St Paul's is at the far end, Jones's arcaded townhouses on the right. The left side, towards the river, was originally open. Painting by John Collet, 1770s.

106 Viola Zanini: interpretation of the Tuscan Temple portico, after Vitruvius, from *Della Architettura*, 1626.

the Queen's Dancing Barne', Jones was marked as a Royalist. He was present at the siege of Basing House, in Hampshire, and after its fall he was carried out with nothing but a blanket to cover him. His estate was confiscated. It had mostly been restored by the time he died at Somerset House on 21 June 1652, aged seventy-eight; but the revolution in architecture he had initiated in England virtually died with him. His circle of influence was restricted to a few initiates in the Office of Works, such as John Webb and Nicholas Stone, but they had neither the authority nor the direct experience of Italy and Roman classicism to sustain the momentum Jones had created.

John Webb (1611–72) was labelled as 'Inigo Jones's man', and when Charles II came to the throne in 1660 he looked set to succeed his master. However, in Restoration England the architectural mood was changing and there were different allegiances. Charles II appointed an architectural lightweight, John Denham, as Surveyor-General instead of Webb. Perhaps as some form of recompense, Webb was given the opportunity to design the King Charles Block at Greenwich Palace, in 1663, and was appointed Surveyor there in 1666. He was certainly familiar with designing on the grand scale, as can be seen from the numerous projects in his hand though under 102 Jones's supervision for the earlier royal palace. The Greenwich block exhibits more his own fascination with Vitruvius's description of the ancient Roman house, which he knew from Jones's annotated copy of the Barbaro *Vitruvius*, the *Quattro libri*, and Scamozzi's *Idea*. Webb's work at Greenwich was absorbed after 1696 into the Naval Hospital, which was built under Christopher Wren, the next Surveyor-General to the King. Webb was sandwiched between two great architects, and was never in a position to exert with any force his own perhaps considerable talents as a Vitruvio-Palladian.

Webb married Anne, Jones's cousin and heir; and he inherited the study of Stonehenge (which he published three years after Jones's 101 death) and the projects for the new royal palace. Wilton House in 107 Wiltshire was also an inheritance of sorts. It had been designed in the 1630s for Philip Herbert, 3rd Earl of Pembroke, by Isaac de Caus (either a son or a nephew of Salomon de Caus), with advice from Inigo Jones. The eventual composition of the south front, which was to prove so influential in 18th-century Palladian architecture, was the result of two accidents. One was the reduction in width of the original design from a megalomaniac twenty-one bays to a more manageable nine; the other was the retention of an earlier (Tudor) tower at the right-hand end, disguised and duplicated to create a front which was

107 De Caus, Jones and Webb: south front of Wilton House, 1630s and 1647–52. The gabled towers and other peculiarly English interpretations of Palladian motifs were highly influential for the British Vitruvians of the next century.

both novel and satisfying and which – by another accident – brought it quite close to a design in Scamozzi's *Idea* that had never been built. In the centre of the façade is another badge of English Palladianism, a Venetian window (though here it has blocked side openings). There was a destructive fire in 1647 and Jones was called in again, but he may have had only a very limited involvement due to his age, and it is assumed that the major task of refurbishment fell to Webb. Some changes were made to the exterior, among them the replacement of gabled roofs on the towers by the present pedimented gables. Inside, the impact of Jones and Webb is still to be felt in the surviving state rooms, notably the famous Double Cube Room – famous as much for its splendid decoration and Van Dyck paintings as for its fine proportions.

The most important inheritance that Webb received, at least for the future of British Palladianism, was Jones's library and collection of drawings by himself and by Italian Renaissance artists. The drawings were mostly dispersed after Webb's death, contrary to his will. Their active re-collection in the early 18th century signalled a new concern for re-establishing the artistic principles which Jones was seen to represent in Britain (see below, p. 155).

146

6 FROM STUARTS TO HANOVERIANS: THE AGE OF
SIR CHRISTOPHER WREN

When the Stuarts returned to power in 1660, the political and intellectual climate was greatly changed, and it was another fifty years before continuity was re-established with the Palladian tradition. A brief account of those fifty years, dominated in architecture by the giant figure of Sir Christopher Wren, is necessary to provide a background for the revival of Palladianism after 1715.

In the eyes of the Parliamentarians, the Stuarts had been guilty of many abuses of their royal authority. Charles I patently misjudged the hostility that his measures were arousing, the growing force of Puritanism, and the desire for free expression. Attempts to curb the power of the press proved ultimately ineffective, and the collapse of censorship not long before the outbreak of the Civil War released a flood of pamphlets and books on a wide range of political, intellectual and religious issues. The appeal to the individual conscience undermined the authority of the monarchy and the Church. Cromwell's Commonwealth imposed its own restrictions, but with the Stuart Restoration both political theory and the natural sciences could be discussed and investigated with a new spirit of independence and a refusal to be bound by dogmas of the past. John Locke laid the foundations of empiricism in philosophy; in medicine, Sir William Harvey's demonstration of the circulation of blood (published in 1628) received wider acclaim; while physics and astronomy made perhaps the greatest strides of all with Newton's formulation of the laws of planetary motion.

From this world of rationality and clear thinking came Sir Christopher Wren (1632–1723). Wren was primarily a mathematician. He was appointed Professor of Astronomy at Gresham College in the City of London at the age of twenty-five. Twelve years later, in 1669, he became Surveyor-General of the King's Works, in succession to Sir John Denham, over the head of John Webb (who missed his chance for the second and last time). Wren seems to have been particularly favoured by Charles II, perhaps because he had spent time in Paris and familiarized himself with the architecture of the French Court, which had sheltered Charles in exile, and partly no doubt because he came from a staunchly Tory, Royalist family. He survived two changes of dynasty, however, in 1688 and 1714, and continued to hold his post until 1718, by which time he was out of fashion architecturally as well as politically.

Wren's own style owes little to French examples, and he absorbed the Italian Renaissance only through books. He was, however, surely influenced by French theoretical writing. The French Academy of Architecture, founded in 1671 by François Blondel, aimed to separate the activities of designing and building and thereby to transform architecture into a profession, whose members were expected not only to possess a thorough knowledge of antique and Renaissance architecture but also to have at least some acquaintance with Gothic and other periods. Wren himself was an example of the narrowing gap between the professional architect and gentleman amateur.

He was certainly well aware of the controversies over aesthetic theory that were going on in France. His own underlying principle was formulated as follows: 'There are two causes of Beauty, Natural and Customary. Natural is from Geometry, consisting in Uniformity (that is Equality) and Proportion. Customary Beauty is begotten by the Use of our Senses.' The former is by far the more important: 'errors', he warns, arise from our prejudices and overfamiliarity with certain forms; and then, 'always the true Test is Natural or Geometrical Beauty'.

108 Gibbs: St Martin-in-the-Fields, London, 1720–26. The design consists of three visually separate elements: the portico, the tiered steeple on a wide base articulated by paired pilasters, and the body of the church with its pilasters and windows framed by rustication.

Wren's architecture can be quite neatly collated with this definition, which also helps to explain some of its apparent contradictions. Renaissance planning, and the proportional systems entailed by the use of the classical orders, have Geometrical Beauty; elements from the medieval tradition can be called Customary. The careful classicism of the west front of St Paul's combines with concealed flying buttresses; the squares, circles and ovals of the City church plans and their classical dress live happily with steeples that are consciously 'modern' versions of Gothic spires.

Something of the same undoctrinaire readiness to compromise can be found in Wren's successors, Nicholas Hawksmoor (1661–1736), Sir John Vanbrugh (1664–1726), Thomas Archer (1668–1723), and James Gibbs (1682–1754). The architecture of the so-called 'English Baroque' does not come within the scope of this book, but it clearly has some bearing on the success of the Neo-Palladian movement that took its place. Hawksmoor and Vanbrugh both evolved styles which, monumental and dramatic as they are, had no progeny. Archer and Gibbs had been to Italy, and Gibbs especially reflects many of the values of Continental Baroque.

The final flourish of the English Baroque under Wren came in 1711, when a Tory Parliament in its final years of government, and

108

with its unerring commitment to the Church, passed an act for the building of fifty churches in London. The supervising Commissioners included Wren, Vanbrugh and Archer, with Hawksmoor and William Dickinson, succeeded by the Scot James Gibbs two years later, as Surveyors. By the time George I was crowned in October 1714, twelve of the churches had been built. With a changing political mood which was becoming increasingly radical, the new monarch had all the commissioners dismissed, retaining only Hawksmoor. James Gibbs, after one year of service, was replaced by John James (the English translator of the most important architectural treatise of the 17th century, *Ordonnance des cinq espèces de colonnes*, written by Claude Perrault in 1683, and translated by James in 1708). His displacement, about which he was naturally bitter, he blamed on the ambitions of an unnamed 'countryman'.

Though Gibbs may have had grounds for discontent, the experience he gained from this brief encounter with the Wren circle was to be useful in the future. He had studied in Rome in the studio of Carlo Fontana and was familiar with the major works of the Italian Baroque which Wren knew only from drawings, and he took up the challenge that Wren had set for churches, of merging traditional features of British church architecture with the sophistications of the Baroque – a hallmark of the Tory establishment. Wren expressed this through the conjunction of two distinctly separate elements, a classical body and 'Gothic' steeple. Gibbs's own version of this appears at St Martin-in-the-Fields in London (1720–26), a design which places all the external symbolism to the front, where a classical portico is surmounted by a tiered steeple. Largely due to its promotion by Gibbs in the plates of his *A Book of Architecture*, published in London in 1728, this somewhat bizarre combination became the symbol of the Anglican establishment in both Britain and the American colonies.

The architecture of Gibbs has a maverick quality about it, and suggests an intellectual independence which makes it difficult to place him in a particular camp. He was a Tory, a Catholic, and part of a fading regime, yet he had an early influence on Lord Burlington who was to become the guiding light of English Neo-Palladianism. Their association, albeit a brief one, provided a link between the English Baroque and the stricter classicism of the emerging British Vitruvians.

Great British Vitruvians

The two political divisions in England, the Tories and the Whigs, embraced many different factions. Broadly speaking, the Tories were pro-monarchy. Many were Royalists accommodated within the parliamentary system; and their detractors branded them as papists for their High-Church loyalties. The Whigs were Parliamentarians, some even Republicans, who were positive Protestants and, in the extreme, Puritans. By the end of the 17th century, after several decades of Tory rule, the Whig party were in the ascendant. Their thinking was dominated by the views of John Locke, who argued that a more enlightened society could better shape itself once freed from the wilful caprices of the monarchy.

Locke's Puritanism was tempered by an inquiring mind, and the *Essay Concerning Human Understanding* (1690) was his attempt at reconciling science with religion. Central to this reconciliation is the discovery of truth through empiricism. For Locke (as for Barbaro a century before), knowledge is a product of experience and observation, aided by reason. Knowledge of God needs to be pursued through these processes and faculties, for 'knowledge', as he asserts repeatedly, 'depends upon the right use of those powers nature hath bestowed on us'. Certain 'truths' central to Lockeian thinking were readily absorbed by the Whigs. Since property was essential to society, so men of property should rule; the sovereignty of Parliament was the sovereignty of the people; the ultimate rule was divine law, though this was to be interpreted by the people – the State – and not the Church. The full effects of this train of thought were to be felt in Revolutionary America, but the high Tory ideals that underpinned Wren's Baroque were the first casualties of the swing to Whig political domination in Britain.

The majority of the Whig party in Parliament in 1715 coincided with the publication of the first volume of *Vitruvius Britannicus*, a beautifully illustrated account of classical architecture in Britain by the Scottish architect Colen Campbell (1676–1729). In April of the same year the young Richard Boyle, 3rd Earl of Burlington (1694– 1753), returned to England from a Grand Tour of Europe, and Italy

119

especially, in time for his twenty-first birthday. He almost immediately began extensions to Burlington House in Piccadilly, London, under the direction of Gibbs (who was probably already involved in modernizing its interior). Gibbs, a master of Italian design, was an obvious choice at that time, but Campbell's publication set new standards which Burlington was determined to address himself. A new artistic era was coming of age with Burlington at its centre. His architectural output, and that of the prime movers of Palladianism closely involved with his new development, are the subject of this section.

I BRITISH VITRUVIANS AND NEO-PALLADIANS

Vitruvius Britannicus was the first book on architecture to have originated in Britain since John Shute's *First Groundes*, 152 years earlier, but it is not a treatise as such. It contains no theoretical commentary on architecture, and the buildings which are presented in the engravings (in the form of plans, sections, elevations, and sometimes even an aerial view of the setting) are given only a paragraph of explanation. Yet while it lacks theory it is not short of opinion: Campbell used his book as a stick with which to beat the Baroque 'excesses' of Wren and High Church Toryism, and decried the influence of Bernini and Gibbs's Italian mentor Carlo Fontana.

Campbell's viewpoint may have been influenced by the Scottish architect James Smith (*c.* 1645–1731), who, by the time Campbell's fame was rising in England, was regarded by some Scots as that nation's most eminent architect. Smith may have been introduced to architecture by travels in Italy in his late twenties. A successful career was almost guaranteed when he married the eldest daughter of Robert Mylne, Master Mason to the Scottish Crown, and Campbell acknowledged him as the 'most experienced Architect' of Scotland in volume II of *Vitruvius Britannicus*. More remarkable than his executed works are his 'fantasy' projects, which show him to have been a closet Palladian: he designed a creditable Rotonda, after Palladio, which appears to have been a direct source for Campbell in his own practice.

Campbell was a Whig, and his dedication of the first volume to the new Hanoverian monarch, George I, together with his opening declaration of the independence of native British genius from both Italy and France, left no doubt that he saw a new age dawning. Wren to his thinking was a genius, but a misguided one. Certainly St Paul's was a worthy challenger to Rome's St Peter's, in size and magnificence, but in Campbell's view the use of classicism in both designs was flawed. He believed he himself held the key to the future, and by placing engravings of these two cathedrals alongside his own project for a great new London church, and his own designs for Wanstead 109–111 House in the company of houses by Jones, Talman, Vanbrugh and Hawksmoor, he stressed the heritage which the British could proudly proclaim their own, whilst drawing attention to his own special talents and aspirations.

Campbell makes the case for British Vitruvio-Palladianism in his introduction. With the noble Grand Tourists in mind, he writes:

The general Esteem that Travellers have for Things that are Foreign, is in nothing more conspicuous than with Regard to Building. We travel, for the most part, at an Age more apt to be imposed upon by the Ignorance or Partiality of others, than to judge truly of the Merit of Things by the Strength of reason. It's owing to this Mistake in Education, that so many of the British Quality have so mean an Opinion of what is performed in our own Country, tho', perhaps, in most we equal, and in some things we surpass, our Neighbours.

He commends the revival of architecture in Italy from Bramante to 'the great' Palladio, 'who has exceeded all that were gone before him'. Since then, however, 'the great Manner and exquisite Taste of Building is lost; for the Italians can no more relish the Antique simplicity, but are entirely employed in capricious Ornaments, which must at last end in the Gothick.' Palladio and 'our Architect' Inigo Jones he regards as showing the way forward; though, with great diplomacy and balance, he does not forget the 'Happiness of the British Nation, that at present abounds with so many learned and ingenious Gentlemen' – like Wren, Vanbrugh, Archer, Talman, Hawksmoor and James.

The first volume was very timely. The Whigs were associated with City merchants and with an aristocratic oligarchy who together were to be responsible for a new era of prosperity. Architecturally, this manifested itself in an increased demand for private house building, which was to be in a style that would express the new self-confident nationalism: the 'antique simplicity' of classical *virtù* was accepted as an ideal. Campbell's plates provide many examples of domestic architecture and very few public and ecclesiastical designs. His enterprise was soon rewarded by Lord Burlington's endorsement of his approach to architecture.

At Burlington House the unfortunate Gibbs seems to have had time only to design a new entrance court and colonnade before being ousted by Campbell – the fellow Scot who had probably been responsible earlier for undermining his appointment to the Church Commission. Campbell absorbed Gibbs's semicircular colonnade into his own design, of which a general plan and main elevation appeared in the third and final volume of *Vitruvius Britannicus* (1725). This elevation gives an indication of the revived simplicity that Campbell sought. It combines the general proposition of Palladio's Palazzo Porto-Colleoni with Jonesian details. Burlington was not content merely to be a patron of the new movement: from the outset he seems to have wanted to determine its course. Most probably he worked closely with Campbell here, and in 1717 he built his own independent design for a 'New Bagnino', or small bath house, in the grounds of his family house at Chiswick near London.

152,162 The year after the publication of Campbell's *Vitruvius Britannicus*, a new translation of the *Quattri libri*, by James Leoni, began to appear. This was a new Palladio in several respects, since it combined a full English translation with specially prepared engravings after Palladio's original woodcuts. James, more correctly Giacomo, Leoni (*c.* 1686–1746) was a Venetian who had arrived in England around 1713. He came via the Palatine court to a nation already highly receptive to Venetian artists. In London he combined his own linguistic abilities with those of an Englishman of French extraction, Nicholas Dubois, who was an architect-engineer. Together they produced a dual English and French translation of the *Quattro libri*. The London-based Venetian painter Sebastiano Ricci designed an allegorical frontispiece, which proclaimed the bright future of Palladianism in England in the reign of George I. The work appeared in instalments between 1716 and 1720, and then as a new edition, in English only, in 1721. Twenty-one years later the last corrected edition included as an Appendix an English version of Palladio's *L'antichità di Roma*, and a transcript of the notes Inigo Jones had made in his 1601 edition of the *Quattro libri*.

The Leoni Palladio was a popular success, but in the eyes of Burlington it was a failure. Leoni had made 'many necessary Corrections' to Palladio's designs, which he considered to be 'an improvement'. Burlington was not sympathetic. To his mind, Leoni had corrupted Palladio's message: his 'corrections' departed from the simplicity of the Vitruvian antique, and were instead an updating of Palladio in the Baroque idiom of Gibbs. Consequently, Leoni was excluded from the Burlington circle and the architectural influence of Campbell remained unrivalled.

Campbell was never reliant on the patronage of Burlington. In 1718 he was appointed deputy to the Surveyor who replaced Wren, William Benson. Wren, by then in his mid-eighties, had been retired out of public service by the new Whig regime, and Campbell was appointed to replace Hawksmoor. Campbell had probably worked with Benson during the building of Wilbury House, Wiltshire, after 1710, which is the earliest example of the Jonesian revival in architecture. Their subsequent partnership was, however, short-lived. Benson survived in his new post for only fifteen months before being dismissed. As Benson's man, Campbell was forced to relinquish his post too, and he left public office in July 1719.

Burlington made his second Italian journey that same year. His principal objective seems to have been to scrutinize the work of Palladio himself, and he spent several months in Vicenza, Venice and elsewhere in the Veneto, studying buildings and acquiring drawings. He bought about sixty drawings by Palladio, mainly of Roman baths, from the incumbents of the Villa Barbaro at Maser. Others he obtained from the Bishop of Verona, and after his return, in 1720–21, he acquired still more, together with drawings by Inigo Jones, from John Talman, son of the architect William Talman. These formed part of Jones's collection, which had been scattered after John Webb's death: they had come to the Talman family through John Oliver, a master mason in the Office of Works. Other drawings remained with the Webb family, and Dr George Clarke, a former member of the Tory Church Commission and a Fellow of All Souls, Oxford, bequeathed a large group to Worcester College in 1736, which includes Jones's copy of the *Quattro libri*. Burlington would have been able to study these collections and, with his recent experience of the buildings and his own considerable corpus of drawings, he had the intellectual and material foundations his intended revival of the classical arts required.

His men of action were also assembled soon after his return to England. These included artists whom he had encountered in Italy, the Italian sculptor Giovanni Battista Guelfi, and the painter William Kent, whom he had met during his first Grand Tour. In addition, he had befriended the poet Alexander Pope, from whom he com-missioned a translation of the *Iliad*, completed in 1720; and he had a long and fruitful association with Handel, who tutored his musical tastes. In 1715, the libretto of Handel's *Amadigi*, by Johan Jakob

Heidegger, had been dedicated to the young Earl, who received rich praise for the direction he had taken: 'The particular Encouragement you have given to the liberal Arts, not only shows the Delicacy of your Taste, but will be a Means to Establish them in this Climate and Italy will no longer boast of being the Seat of Politeness, whilst the Sons of Art flourish under your Patronage.'

It is as if Burlington had been consciously responding to the ideal of *noblesse oblige* expressed by the Earl of Shaftesbury in his *Soliloquy: or, Advice to an Author* (1710). Shaftesbury had determined the leadership role the intellectual élite should take on if the arts and sciences were to flourish once the liberty of the people had been wrested from the monarchy: 'In a Government where the people are sharers in Power, but no Distributers or Dispensers of Rewards, they expect it of their Princes and Great Men, that they should supply the generous Part.' It was up to men like Burlington to strive to re-create the benevolent order of the Universe on earth through the exercise of reason on social order. The individual must display his virtue and act as a 'moral artist', or as 'a second *Maker*; a just Prometheus, under Jove'. Shaftesbury, a pupil and supporter of Locke, had been a tremendous force for change through his many writings, and had done much to engender a sense of national self-confidence in the arts. Not that he was a chauvinist. Indeed, he was an ardent admirer of the Virgilian landscapes painted by Poussin. But he lamented the direction that the arts in Britain had taken latterly, and considered that Wren misapplied his talents: 'The Genius of our Nation has hitherto been so little turned this way, that thro' several reigns we have patiently seen the noblest buildings perish (if I may say so) under the hand of a single Court-Architect.'

Campbell's introductory plea in *Vitruvius Britannicus* reflected Shaftesbury's appeal, and his own efforts in architecture and architectural publishing set new standards which galvanized aristocrats, landed gentlemen, and city professionals to build on the classical heritage of Britain.

Campbell's own very grand version of the Palladian villa appeared in the first volume of *Vitruvius Britannicus*, as a presentation of two alternative designs for Wanstead House in Essex, for Sir Richard Child, heir to an East Indian fortune. The size of the proposed building suggests a palace rather than a villa. The first design is a 200-foot-long rectangular block, having a central hexastyle portico   109
flanked on either side by six windows. This was rejected by Child in favour of a still larger building, 260 feet long, with a heightened   110
central element flanked by lower wings. Common to both designs is a giant Composite order supporting a pediment which rises above the upper cornice balustrade and extends back as a double-pitched roof to present a pedimented gable on the garden elevation. Wanstead II, however, has an additional roofscape element in the form of a cupola, which reveals its author's debt to Vanbrugh's Castle Howard garden elevation, shown in the same volume. The house was built, without a cupola, in 1713–20. Later, in his volume III (1725), Campbell published a further revision of the design, this time proposing to   111
terminate the elevations with four visually stabilizing corner towers, each with a Venetian window – a design which by then had been closely realized at Houghton.   115

The immediate antecedents of Wanstead II are to be found in the late 17th-century country houses of the Wren circle, but the 'simplicity' that Campbell sought was influenced by the Jonesian south front of Wilton House. Campbell's message was received loud   107
and clear: Vanbrugh, for example, though he did not embrace Palladianism wholeheartedly, toned down his elevations for Grimsthorpe Castle in Lincolnshire.

Wanstead was followed by two smaller houses. Stourhead in Wiltshire was begun in 1721 as a country retreat for the banker Henry Hoare. It is a canonical example of the tripartite Palladian villa format, consisting of a compact block with a basement, principal floor and attic, with a portico flanked on either side by a single window. In plan it is close to the central block of Palladio's Villa Emo at Fanzolo: a more or less square shell is divided into three – a broader central section corresponding to the width of the portico, containing in sequence the hall, stairs and saloon; and narrower side sections corresponding to the single bays flanking the portico and containing smaller rooms. In 1723 Henry Herbert, later 9th Earl of Pembroke (c. 1689–1750), commissioned a town-house from Campbell in   112

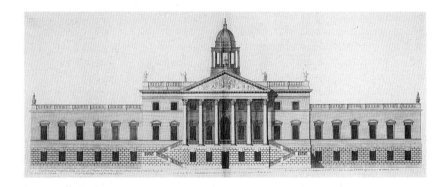

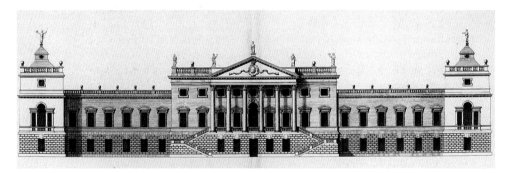

109–111 Campbell: alternative designs for the entrance front of Wanstead House. Wanstead II was the design built in 1713–20, though without the flamboyant cupola. From *Vitruvius Britannicus*, II, 1717 (Wanstead I and II), and III, 1725 (Wanstead III).

112 *opposite* Campbell: house for Lord Herbert, Whitehall, London, 1723. From *Vitruvius Britannicus*, III, 1725.

Whitehall, London, which was designed as a variation on the Stour-head format. At Stourhead the tall portico embraces the *piano nobile* and the attic, and is entered directly from the ground by two side staircases. (Campbell had originally provided two designs, for both attached and freestanding porticoes; the former was built, but it was replaced about 1840 by a variant of the latter.) In Lord Herbert's town-house the portico functions more as a grand balcony to the   112 principal floor and has no external access. The entrance is below, in the centre of the rusticated base. A source for this arrangement may have been an early design by Inigo Jones for the Queen's House at Greenwich, dated 1616.

Lord Herbert was five years older than Burlington and was a legitimate heir to English Palladianism as the incumbent of Wilton. Like Burlington, he was inspired by Campbell to practise architecture himself, and the house in Whitehall was the basis for his first building, Marble Hill at Twickenham, begun in 1724 for the Countess of   132 Suffolk. This he designed with the assistance of Roger Morris (1695–1749), a master carpenter.

113–115 Campbell's next major design was for Houghton in Norfolk, under the patronage of Sir Robert Walpole, the Whig prime minister. As early as 1717, Campbell had inscribed to Walpole a design for a 100-foot-square house linked by galleries to two side buildings, which would, he explained, 'introduce the *Temple* Beauties in a private Building'. In 1722 he began Houghton as a half-scale version of this design, with four corner towers similar to those he later 111 proposed for Wanstead III. Two square dependencies, a kitchen and a laundry court, are linked to the main building by two quarter-circle colonnades – a version of Palladio's Villa Thiene-type layout, of which several examples had been built in Britain since its introduction at Stoke Bruerne almost a century before. Campbell was dismissed before the building was completed, however, and Gibbs (who may have been involved earlier as well) placed high octagonal domes on the unfinished end towers, instead of the gabled 'houses' Campbell

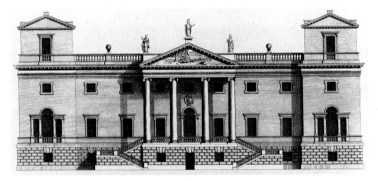

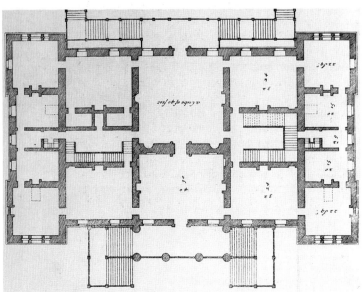

Campbell: Houghton Hall, begun 1722.

113, 114   Proposed elevation of the garden front, where the temple portico becomes an architectural element in the landscape, and plan of the principal floor (shown inverted, with the garden front at the bottom). From *Vitruvius Britannicus*, III, 1725.

115   *opposite* The entrance front, as completed by Gibbs *c.* 1729.

had proposed: sweet revenge, perhaps, for the past injustices he believed he had suffered because of Campbell.

Campbell used a Jonesian Ionic on the exterior, with angled volutes and a pulvinated frieze, and the room proportions are unmistakably Jonesian too. The main hall, for instance, is a 40-foot cube, the same as that at the Queen's House. The overall composition of the elevation derives from Wilton. The heavily rusticated surrounds of the 107 windows on the entrance front are of a type found in Webb's Greenwich block, and derived from the Palazzo Thiene; their 17 application to the Venetian windows at the ends is a curious invention of Campbell's own. The rear of the house is plainer, with an applied Ionic portico. A freestanding portico, reminiscent of those in the Wanstead designs, was intended, but both that and the external stairs shown in Campbell's plates remained unrealized.

The appearance of Houghton is a blend of English architectural ideas, from Wilton to Wanstead. Campbell was not rejecting outright the influence of Palladio, as the title of *Vitruvius Britannicus* might seem to suggest, but he did not feel dependent on or intimidated by the Italian master. This is clear from his most overtly Palladian house, Mereworth Castle in Kent. Built in 1722–25 for John Fane, later Earl 116–118 of Westmorland, this is an essay on the Villa Rotonda theme. Unlike 56 the Rotonda and Scamozzi's Rocca Pisani, which stand on high 81 ground with commanding views, it is situated low down in a river valley, on the foundations of a former castle; but like them it was intended as a retreat. Campbell was concerned that his design should not be seen as a mere copy. To this end, in *Vitruvius Britannicus* he draws attention to the differences between Mereworth and the Rotonda, not the superficial similarities. 'The new Plan', he points out, 'is much enlarged, and the Ground Story intirely different' (III, 61,116

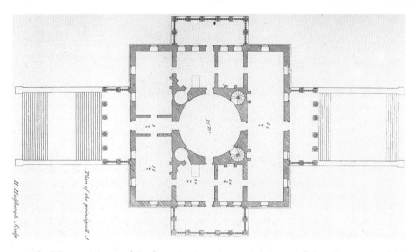

p. 8). He continues his description as a criticism of the Rotonda: his design permits more light to enter the interiors; there is a wider variety of room sizes; the porticoes are open at the sides; circular stairs instead of triangular ones allow door openings to be aligned geometrically; Portland stone is used to ornament the building whereas the original is in brick and stucco with a wooden entablature; and – apparently confusing the Rotonda design with Scamozzi's plate of the Rocca Pisani – he states that Palladio's building had just four chimneys in the form of obelisks, whereas Mereworth has twenty-four flues collected at the lantern under a copper 'callot'.

A Rotonda-like design by James Smith may have had some influence on Mereworth, especially on Campbell's preference for circular stairs, but in accordance with Vitruvian demands, Campbell's design has more *utilitas* than that of his fellow Scot, as well as more *firmitas* (as he was at pains to point out to his readers) than the Rotonda of Palladio. On the *venustas*, beauty, of his projects he remained silent – a humility which was entirely appropriate considering that by the time of this publication his noble and influential patron, Lord Burlington, was exercising his own talent for architecture.

Burlington was particularly active during the 1720s. He began Tottenham Park in Wiltshire for his brother-in-law, Lord Bruce, in 1722 (using the Wilton corner towers motif), and Warwick House in London. He also built adjoining town-houses in London for Lord Mountrath (*c.* 1721) and General Wade. The latter was an almost direct copy of an unpublished drawing by Palladio in Burlington's collection. His most innovative Vitruvio-Palladian experiments were, however, at Chiswick and York.

80

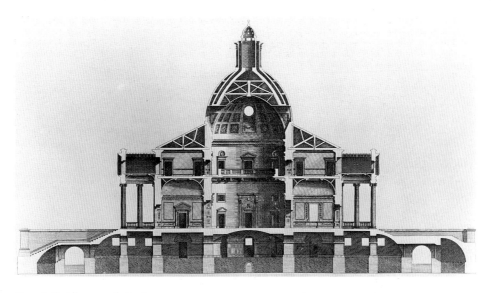

Campbell: Mereworth Castle, 1722–25.

116, 117 Plan of the principal floor and section on the same axis, with the entrance portico on the left. From *Vitruvius Britannicus*, III, 1725.

118 View from the entrance side.

Earl of Burlington

119   Portrait of Lord Burlington by Jonathan Richardson, *c.* 1717–19.

The Scamozzi chimney-obelisks of which Campbell was critical were very acceptable to Lord Burlington in his design for a villa next to his Jacobean house at Chiswick near London, begun *c.* 1725. The villa has a generic link with both the Rotonda and the Rocca Pisani. The plans of Chiswick and the Rotonda are both 68 feet square, though the difference between the two units means that Burlington's design is about 3.5 metres smaller than the Rotonda: 68 Vicentine feet (V.ft) and 68 English feet (E.ft) equal 24.30 and 20.73 metres, respectively.

Burlington was concerned with the numbers that regulate the spaces, and he shows a preference for integers whenever it proves practical. The largest rectangular rooms in the Rotonda measure 26×15 V.ft; Burlington uses the same numbers for the Red and Green Velvet Rooms, and gives them a height of 20 E.ft instead of the precise mean proportional of $20\frac{1}{2}$ – an approximation permitted by Palladio. But apart from these Palladian correspondences, Chiswick Villa is closer to Scamozzi's Rocca Pisani and Serlio's reinterpretation of the Odeo Cornaro in his Book VII. Serlio's octagonal central space and four circular stairs reappear at Chiswick, though here the space is again smaller and the side niches are omitted. Serlio's square-headed lantern windows become thermal windows at Chiswick, and the lantern is covered by a saucer-shaped dome like that of the Rocca Pisani. The garden elevation has a triplet of Venetian windows, each inscribed in an arch, a motif taken directly from a drawing by Palladio, while the side elevations have a single central Venetian window, as has the Rocca Pisani. The entrance front of Chiswick includes Serlio's and Palladio's single windows with triangular pediments.

The staircases that lead up to the balustraded hexastyle portico on the entrance front are perhaps Burlington's most original contribution to this mélange of sources. They are similar to those built at Wanstead and proposed for Houghton, but more elaborate: on either side two flights, not one, lead up from the ground; and at the level of the half-landings, which align with the principal windows, additional flights are inserted, a somewhat excessive gesture for the small scale of the building. No wonder Lord Hervey protested when he first saw the villa: 'House! Do you call it a house? Why! it is too little to live in, and too large to hang on one's watch.'

Inside Chiswick Villa the rooms are more varied in shape than those of the Rotonda, and recall the plans Palladio made of Roman baths.

80

120–122

61

80,81

58

110,113

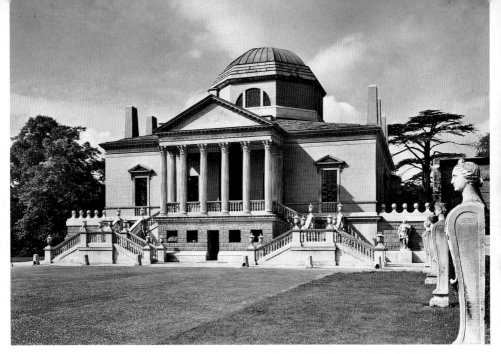

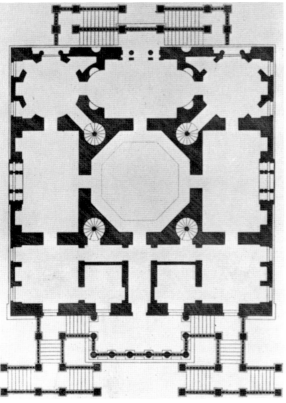

Burlington: Chiswick Villa, begun *c.* 1725.

120 Entrance front.

121 Plan of the principal floor, with the ornate staircases at the lower edge. From Kent, *The Designs of Inigo Jones*, 1727.

122 *opposite* The garden front, with its triplet of Venetian windows. The chimney-obelisks and domed centre were inspired by Scamozzi's representation of his own Rocca Pisani (see Ill. 80).

The most complex and remarkable sequence of spaces is at the rear, where a central rectangular room terminating in niched apses is flanked by a circular room and an octagonal room. These and the other rooms are richly ornamented and have fireplaces taken from examples by Jones.

Burlington was prepared to experiment freely with the vocabulary of Serlio, Palladio and Jones in the grounds of his own house, but his surviving public building in York is more chaste and conveys a purer 123–126 Vitruvian ideal, appropriate to the ancient city the Romans called Eboracum. In May 1730, Burlington was requested by the city fathers to design 'a large Dancing Room, not less than 90 ft long, another large room for cards and play, another for Coffee and Refreshments and a kitchen or place to make Tea in, with a retiring place for the ladies. And somewhere about the entrance, perhaps underground, a place with a chimney for footmen . . .' On 1 March 1731, the foundation stone of the Assembly Rooms was laid, inscribed with the building's programme: a 'place for public pastime where the liberal arts should flourish and where the new splendour should emulate the ancient glory of Eboracum'.

This glory was to be emulated in a structure related to Vitruvius' description of the 'Egyptian Hall', which Palladio had illustrated in

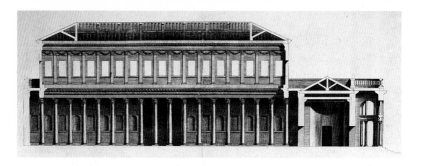

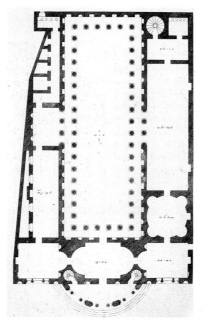

Burlington: Assembly Rooms, York,
1731–32.

123–125 Longitudinal section,
original façade (note how the side
rooms, curved central entrance screen,
and double-height main hall are each
expressed quite distinctly), and plan.
From Woolfe and Gandon, *Vitruvius
Britannicus*, I, 1767.

126 *opposite* Interior

the *Quattro libri* and had described as 'suitable for festivals and entertainments'. The Egyptian Hall is similar in arrangement to the Basilica, with colonnaded aisles and a clerestory, but differs from it in that the colonnade runs round all four sides, and the aisles are narrower. Burlington drew from Palladio's representation of both Roman types, referring to the cross-section and partial plan of the Egyptian Hall six columns wide, and the Basilica plan eighteen columns long, as they appear in the *Quattro libri*. Consequently, the principal room has a plan proportion of 1:3, a compromise which suited the narrow site and the building's intended use; though this proportion is contrary to Vitruvius' recommendation for the Egyptian Hall which he likened to a dining room, having a length twice its width. Burlington invented a highly original façade (since replaced), using his collection of drawings by Palladio of Roman baths, with a convexly curved centre and flanking wings, all pierced by double-height arched openings that combine a thermal window above with a tripartite screen below.

The rigour with which Burlington exploited this Vitruvio-Palladian *idea* was not matched in his concern for the convenience of the users of the building. Whilst it was generally acclaimed, and an overrun in cost was brushed aside by its supporters, there were serious objections about the narrow intervals between the columns (awkward at a time when wide panniered dresses were the fashion) and the placing of the seating in the constricted aisles behind the screen of columns. Both problems were overcome by moving the seating forward to the line of the colonnades.

30

124

The York Assembly Rooms were entirely the conception of Burlington, who followed Vitruvian architectural principles and adapted them to modern use. It is likely that William Kent (1685–1748), who had been living in Burlington's household since he was invited there from Italy in 1720, had little or no impact on the architectural formulation of any of the early projects. A decade later, however, Kent was undoubtedly collaborating closely with his patron on design and execution.

Kent had initially been promoted by Burlington as a history painter, using the skills he had obtained in the Rome studio of Luti to paint scenes from classical mythology. Burlington succeeded in ousting the established London painter Sir James Thornhill from Kensington Palace, where he was decorating the interior, and installed Kent in his place. Kent's wallpaintings took six years to complete, from 1721 to 1727, during which time he was also engaged on decorative programmes at Houghton Hall, and at Chiswick on Burlington's behalf. He turned out to be something of a disappointment as a painter, but the Earl remained faithful to him, and redirected his talents towards architecture.

Horace Walpole referred to Burlington in glowing terms as 'the Apollo of Arts' and to Kent as 'his proper priest'. In several of his earlier projects, Burlington had used a Clerk of Works, Samuel Savill, with Henry Flitcroft as his draughtsman. By the early 1730s Kent was able to perform both these roles, for by then he had received a thorough training in architectural design and construction. From about 1724 onwards he had been given the task by Burlington of editing drawings by Inigo Jones (and John Webb); these appeared in 121,155 1727 as *The Designs of Inigo Jones*, with engraved plates based on re-drawings of the originals by Henry Flitcroft. In 1726 he was appointed Master Carpenter in the Office of Works, rising over the next nine years to hold the joint offices of Master Mason and Deputy Surveyor, positions which he retained for the remainder of his life. In 1734, a year before this double appointment, work was begun on Holkham Hall, Norfolk, a project on which Burlington and Kent collaborated, though the extent of their contribution to its design is unclear.

127–129 Holkham was built for the Whig Earl of Leicester, who, as Thomas Coke, had toured northern Italy twenty years earlier, during the summer and autumn of 1714. In the meantime he had built up a collection of antiquities, and he required an appropriate setting to house them. According to the local supervising architect, Matthew Brettingham, the starting-point for the design of Holkham was Palladio, and his Villa Trissino at Meledo and Villa Mocenigo, though its origins are undoubtedly more complex.

Lord Leicester had been considering plans for a new house since the early 1720s, and Campbell produced a design in 1724, of which no details survive. However, in 1726, Brettingham drew up plans and elevations under Leicester's supervision which resemble Campbell's designs for the neighbouring Houghton Hall. At this stage the influence of Burlington also appears, since the portico and staircases Brettingham drew are similar to those at Chiswick, as are the Venetian windows under enclosing arches. A few years later four wings were added to the design, and building commenced in 1734.

Most of the surviving drawings are by Brettingham and are annotated by Lord Leicester. However, the influence of Burlington and Campbell pervades the final building. The overall composition of Holkham's plan – a central house, with four wing buildings, two on   127
either side defining courts – resembles Burlington's Tottenham Park, which was started in 1722 and developed into the 1730s. Yet the wings at Holkham are more regular, and the elevational details, apparently derived from Chiswick, are better composed. There are elevation drawings by Kent of the entry and garden fronts which develop the earlier drawings by Brettingham. Apart from varying the surface textures, from highly rusticated to smooth, Kent retained the 'Burlingtonian' form of Venetian window drawn by Brettingham. In the end, the enclosing arches were eliminated from the windows of the garden front, though the hexastyle portico of Kent's design remained.

The garden front of Holkham is also very close to Campbell's   128
published design for the garden front of Houghton. Even the plan of   113
the main house is very similar to Houghton's, except for two major   114
differences: there is a great apsidal hall where Campbell had placed his Jonesian cubic hall, and to the west of the hall a gallery sequence instead of bedrooms. There are drawings by Kent which determine the character of the hall, though its overall form had apparently been determined by Leicester. The gallery probably came from Burlington. Chiswick includes a sequence of three variously shaped   121
rooms which are independent of the rectilinear structural walls, and the Holkham gallery sequence consists of similar geometrical episodes.

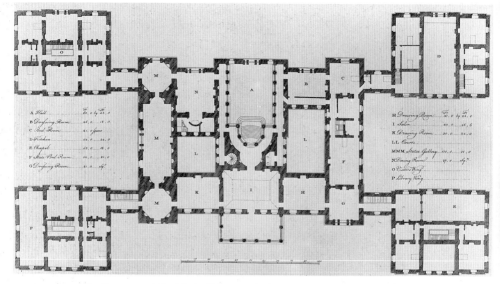

Burlington and Kent?: Holkham Hall, begun 1734.

127 Plan of the principal floor. From Woolfe and Gandon, *Vitruvius Britannicus*, II, 1771.

129 *opposite* The Marble Hall, completed 1764. Beyond the door lies the saloon; other rooms are reached via the galleries at the sides.

128 Garden front.

The decoration that Kent provided for these and other rooms in the house is bold and architectural in character. Authentic Roman details – probably chosen by Leicester – were taken from plates in Palladio and in Antoine Desgodetz's *Les Edifices antiques de Rome* (1682). The Saloon, for example, has a Composite entablature adapted from Palladio, and a coved ceiling with coffering after Desgodetz's rendering of the Basilica of Maxentius; the Marble Hall has an Ionic order based on that of the Temple of Fortuna Virilis.

63

129
30, 126

The Marble Hall at Holkham owes something both to the Roman Basilica, with its apse, and to the Egyptian Hall idea that Burlington had explored at York. Here, though, it serves not only for entertainments but as a circulation space, up and through the house, leading forward to the Saloon and thence towards the garden. The space focuses on a stair which is integrated into the plan in a semicircular apse at the end, conveniently out of the way of the rectangular hall: this apsed arrangement was part of the early Leicester-Brettingham design. Provision is made for musicians and onlookers in the two upper galleries, which also serve as corridors. The overall effect is more theatrical and scenographic than the York Assembly Rooms, and its formal and spatial complexity is heightened by the illusionistic coved ceiling. Kent's painterly approach may have been influential here, though the semicircle of columns enclosing the apse is

50

reminiscent of the screen to the choir of Palladio's Redentore, which had been much admired by Burlington. The space is redolent of Vitruvian antiquity, which was entirely appropriate as a setting for Lord Leicester, who was perhaps the greatest collector of Roman antiquities in Britain since Lord Arundel in the days of Inigo Jones. The impressive antique quality of this hall was not matched until Robert Adam built Kedleston some forty years later.

Even with his knowledge of antiquity and design, it would be unreasonable to assume that Leicester could have conceived and built Holkham with only the help of Brettingham, and that the contribution of Burlington and Kent was marginal. Such maturity is not easily won. Even without hard evidence supporting Burlington's involvement his mark is everywhere and, with Campbell's death in 1729, he remains the most probable coordinator of this large and very successful enterprise.

Burlington's ability to manipulate the form of a large-scale urban project in the Palladian style was soon to be tested. The position of authority that Kent held in the Office of Works gave the design partnership a series of opportunities in London for some major public

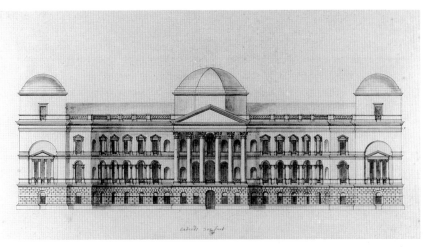

130   Burlington and Kent: design for new Houses of Parliament in London,
1739. On either side of the central portico the building would have curved
forward in two quadrants to Old Palace Yard.

projects. In 1732, Kent produced drawings for new Houses of
Parliament, a building which, given the greater power of that
institution, had a status equivalent to that of the proposed Whitehall
Palace which Inigo Jones had mooted for the Stuarts. The Parliament
building was intended to symbolize national unity and the power of
the State. Burlington's involvement in the form it should take was
acknowledged quite openly. James Ralph, in his *Critical Review of the
Publick Buildings in London* (1734), observed that if Burlington's
'noble hands' were to contribute to the design 'there is no room to
doubt but that the grandeur of this appearance will answer the
majestick purposes 'tis to be employ'd in.'

A final design for the new Parliament, dated 1739, has all the   130
hallmarks of Burlington's influence. There is a central element
crowned by an octagonal stepped saucer dome of the Chiswick Villa
mould, and towers at the ends with thermal windows on their upper
storeys. The principal floor is articulated by a series of Venetian
windows. The most novel element in the design is the portico–like
windows, in which a pediment is supported by four colonnettes.
These do not occur in any building by Palladio, but they may derive
from a sketch design of his for a palace.

By the end of the 1730s the Vitruvio-Palladianism of Burlington and Kent had become a generally recognized formula: a simply delineated building profile, often composed of a dominant centre and secondary wings, and perforated by Palladian elements disposed to complement the overall composition. The Venetian window, a favourite motif, was often placed at either end of a façade composition, which might also be marked by towers; the combination of such windows with towers is an entirely English preference, without precedent in the work of Palladio. For the next generation of Palladians Burlington's formula became increasingly caricatured, a stylistic shorthand disassociated from the high values with which Burlington and his circle were concerned. Alexander Pope captured the dilemma of Palladianism in his *Epistle to Lord Burlington*, originally composed in 1731. Applauding the vision of his patron, he decried its impoverishment by 'imitating fools':

> You show us, Rome was glorious, not profuse,
> And pompous Buildings once were things of use.
> Just as they are, yet shall your noble Rules,
> Fill half the land with Imitating Fools;
> Who random Drawings from your Sheets shall take,
> And of one Beauty many Blunders make;
> Load some vain Church with old Theatric State,
> Turn Arcs of Triumph to a Garden-gate;
> Reverse your Ornaments, and hang them all
> On some patch'd Dog hole ek'd with Ends of Wall;
> Then clap four slices of Pilaster on't,
> And, lac'd with bits of Rustic, 'tis a front
> Shall call the Winds thro' long Arcades to roar
> Proud to catch cold at a Venetian door;
> Conscious they act a true Palladian part,
> And if they starve, they starve by Rules of Art.
> Yet thou proceed; be fallen Arts thy care,
> Erect new Wonders, and the Old repair,
> Jones and Palladio to themselves restore,
> And be whate'er Vitruvius was before . . .

Burlington had been successful in propagating a Vitruvio-Palladian architecture without being a prolific builder. Important in this respect was the rise in architectural publishing, which was

131 Kent and Vardy: Horse Guards, Whitehall, London, 1751–58.

encouraged by Burlington even though he was not always involved directly. He himself seems to have been concerned to keep the new movement faithful to Palladio, but those outside his influence modernized and popularized his message. Leoni's translation of the *Quattro libri* is a case in point (see above, p. 154).

Several alternatives to Leoni's unreliable Palladio were produced. Colen Campbell found time to begin an edition of his own, but only the *First Book* was completed and printed in 1728, a year before his death. The next edition was marginally preferable to Leoni's: Edward Hoppus and Benjamin Cole merely cobbled together re-engravings of Book I as published by Campbell, with Leoni's Books II–IV tagged onto the end. This came out as *Andrea Palladio's Architecture in Four Books . . . Carefully Revis'd and Redelineated* between 1733 and 1735. It 142 was not until 1738 that the definitive English-language edition of the *Quattro libri* was published. By Isaac Ware, it was 'literally translated from the original Italian' and had extremely accurate copper-plate-engraved copies of the original woodcuts in 'the Author's own hand'. This work was dedicated to Burlington, whose own active contribution Ware acknowledged.

Whilst the Ware edition met Burlington's exacting requirements, its publication was ill-timed. The initial flush of Palladian revival was over by the late 1730s, and the Leoni edition had been accepted for too long by too many to be dismissed as an irrelevance. Coupled with this, Burlington was withdrawing from architectural practice and becoming less of a leading light. Kent, who continued in the Office of Works, became less accountable to Burlington and began to investigate alternatives to Palladianism. His Horse Guards building in 131

177

Whitehall, executed after his death by John Vardy in 1751–58, combines aspects of an early Holkham design with a skyline more evocative of Gibbs or even the early Jacobean style of Inigo Jones. Kent had also become increasingly interested in a romantic notion of the Age of Chivalry, as his illustrations for Spenser's *Faerie Queene* (1751) suggest. Robert Walpole had encouraged Kent to abandon the classical mode when rebuilding part of the Tudor Clock Court at Hampton Court in the 1730s, and Kent invented a 'Gothick' choir screen for Gloucester Cathedral in 1741 (since removed).

Ultimately, while the Burlington circle formed the nucleus of the Palladian revival in England, in the American colonies their importance was diffused by pattern books and handbooks on building – practical manuals which made sense of high architectural aims for the benefit of craftsmen and their patrons. These books were distributed widely and were taken as the main indicators of the architecture of the post-Wren era in England. One of the most successful authors was Michael Hoare, alias William Halfpenny (d. 1775), who wrote easily comprehensible handbooks on classical detailing. First came *Practical Architecture* (*c.* 1720), intended for 'those who are engaged in ye noble art of building'. This was followed by *Magnum in Parvo, or the Marrow of Architecture* (1722), designed for young gentlemen to understand the rules 'tho' an utter stranger to ye art', and technical manuals on building and perspective. Another popular author was Batty Langley (1696–1751), who published over twenty books on gardening and building.

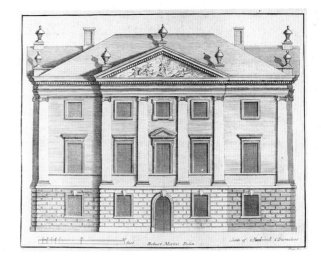

132 Lord Herbert and Roger Morris: Marble Hill, Twickenham, 1724–26.

133 Robert Morris: design for a house based on Marble Hill, from *An Essay in Defence of Ancient Architecture*, 1728.

There were more ambitious publications which combined practical information with theory. Marble Hill House at Twickenham was 132 the centre of an important account of Palladian design theory published by Robert Morris (1701–54), a kinsman of Roger Morris who had assisted Lord Herbert in its design. Without naming the building, Robert Morris offered its plan and elevation as an example 133 of the true application of ancient principles. Morris put forward his thesis in *An Essay in Defence of Ancient Architecture* (1728). He favoured a return to the 'Beauty and Harmony' of the ancients, as opposed to the 'Irregularity' of modern architecture, by which he meant principally the work of the Vanbrugh-Hawksmoor school. Like Campbell, Morris wished to regain the simplicity of the Palladian approach to architecture, but more than Campbell he provided a system of rules by which such an ideal might readily be achieved.

Lectures on Architecture. Consisting of Rules Founded upon Harmonick and Arithmetical Proportions in Building Design'd as an Agreeable Entertainment for Gentlemen, published in London in 1734, proved to be more than a humble diversion for gentlemen: it was a guide to harmonic proportion and geometry which made the Palladian movement more generally accessible. Morris's basic proportional scheme for the design of a house is derived from a cube subdivided into smaller 'cubic' modules. Preferred dimensions for rooms are multiples of the module, which is also used to determine the size and position of every element, from windows to chimneybreasts, subjecting the entire composition to a coordinated rigour. Similarly, the

179

façade is subdivided into three horizontal bands: the basement, which is preferably rusticated; then two floors of accommodation unified by a giant order, chosen to suit the building's use and location. Morris explained his system of proportion as a lesson learnt from nature through the medium of music, which leads to rules of 'Arithmetical Harmony'. Thus, 'The Square in Geometry, the Unison or Circle in Music and the Cube in Building have all an inseparable Proportion; the Parts being equal . . . give the Eye and Ear an agreeable Pleasure, from hence may likewise be deduc'd the Cube and half, the Double Cube; the Diapason and Diapente, being founded on the same Principles in Musick.' The second part of the book, dedicated to Roger Morris, his master 'both in theory and practice', shows how these simple rules may be applied to designing houses. Morris followed these personal accounts of Vitruvian and Palladian theory with two pattern books, *Rural Architecture* (1750) and *The Architectural Remembrancer* (1751). Whereas comparable works by Batty Langley had been aimed at the building trade directly, Morris's were pitched at the gentleman and amateur architect, and their content was highly accessible; they also provided a practical starting-point in America where there was no body of professional architects. *Rural* 138,149 *Architecture* was republished in 1755 and 1757 as *Select Architecture*, which proved very popular in America for its plans and elevations of country houses. The most eminent gentleman-architect there to scrutinize its pages was Thomas Jefferson, and it is in America that the Palladianism of Jones and Burlington is continued, for in England, after 1750, the movement drifted into the rigours of Neoclassicism, a reinterpretation of Greek as well as Roman antiquity.

134   Robert Morris: double cube house in the Corinthian mode, 1735 – published in his *Lectures on Architecture* (1734 etc.) and *Rural Architecture* (1750).

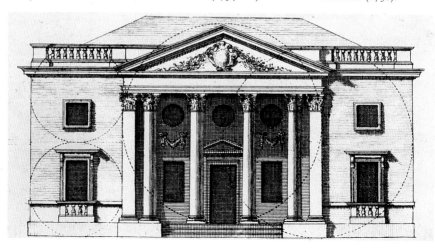

PART SIX

Anglo-Palladianism and the birth of a new nation

I   THE EARLY CLASSICAL VERNACULAR IN AMERICA

During the eighteenth century, settlements along the eastern seaboard of America became increasingly established and prosperous, and with rising wealth and development buildings became correspondingly grander. Most pre-18th-century buildings were in a timber vernacular, and more durable but expensive materials like brick were used sparingly, usually for chimney stacks. Even in the early 18th century most bricks came from England, and arrived in America as ballast in underladen merchant ships on their return voyage westward. Much of the building expertise had to be brought from England as well, especially fine joiners and carpenters. Without the direction of architects, these men were free to work as their experience informed them. General designs and details were available from English pattern-books and these were referred to in lieu of expert advice.

The architecture of the Wren era in England established itself as the most fashionable style: and 'style' it was, for there was no concern for profound theories of beauty and culture in early colonial America. It is therefore perhaps not surprising that at first Leoni's translation of Palladio did not effect a dramatic change in taste, and that Gibbs's *A Book of Architecture* of over a decade later was better received. Gibbs's architecture was closer to the Wren style to which builders were accustomed, and was intended to be

of use to such Gentlemen as might be concerned in building, especially in the remote parts of the Country, where little or no assistance for Design can be procured. Such may here be furnished with Draughts of useful and convenient Buildings and proper Ornaments which may be executed by any Workman who understands Lines, either as here Design'd, or with some Alteration, which may be easily made by a person of Judgement . . .

The *Book* was an architectural best-seller, and Gibbs's design for St Martin-in-the Fields in London became a standard for churches down the east coast.   108

Virginian planters favoured the establishment authority of the Wren-Baroque familiar to them through the architecture of their provincial capital Williamsburg, and well into the second half of the 18th century the influence of Gibbs was still prevalent. At Mount Airy (*c.* 1758), Richmond County, the plan and river front of the house are taken from *A Book of Architecture*. A native Virginian, John Ariss (*c.* 1725–1799), is usually credited as the builder, and he is associated with other houses built between 1758 and 1762. Ariss, according to an advertisement in the *Maryland Gazette* in 1751, was 'lately from Great Britain' and was prepared to undertake 'Buildings of all Sorts and Dimensions . . . either of the ancient or Modern Order of Gibbs'. Palladianism in the form of Robert Morris's *Select Architecture* appears

136,137

135

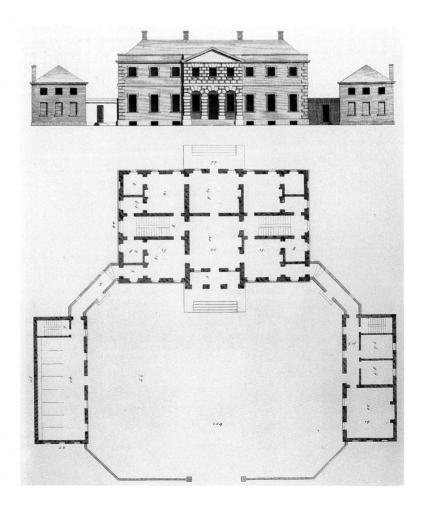

135   *opposite* Gibbs: elevation and plan of a country house, from *A Book of Architecture*, 1728.

136, 137   *above and below* John Ariss: Mount Airy, Richmond County, Virginia, *c.* 1758. View and plan.

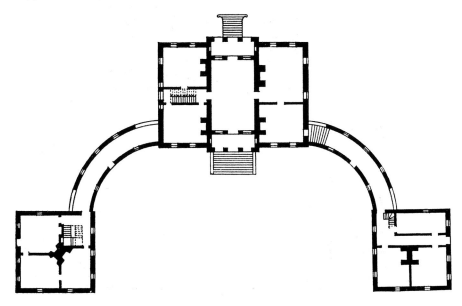

141   Drayton Hall, South Carolina, 1738–42.

138   *opposite top* Robert Morris: elevation and plan of a country house, from *Select Architecture*, 1755.

139, 140   *opposite middle and bottom* Brandon, Prince George County, Virginia, *c*. 1765, view and plan.

at Battersea and at Brandon, Virginia, both after a country house   139,140
design by Morris. These were built in the early and mid-1760s,   138
respectively, a few years after the publication of *Select Architecture*.

Further south, where the climate is closer to that of the Italian
Veneto, the Palladian villa-type proved ideal to cope with the long
hot humid summers which plantation owners had to endure. Here
there was no risk of catching 'cold at a Venetian door', of which
Alexander Pope had complained: on the contrary, porticoes provided
the welcome shade for which they were designed. In isolated and
apparently unrelated locations Palladian illustrations from the *Four
Books* were imitated closely, as if that too were no more than a
pattern-book. The Villa Pisani at Montagnana was the general model
for Drayton Hall, built in 1738–42, near Charleston in South Carolina.   141
Mount Clare, at Baltimore in Maryland, built after 1760, is a blend of
the Villas Saraceno and Zen, combined with details probably taken
from a workaday pattern-book: *Practical Architecture* by William
Halfpenny, of *c*. 1720.

142 Temple-fronted garden pavilion, from Hoppus and Cole, *Andrea Palladio's Architecture in Four Books*, 1733–35.

The most noted 'architect' of this time was Peter Harrison (1716–75), who was based in Rhode Island: he was the first true interpreter of Anglo-Palladianism in America. Born in York, England, he had emigrated to Newport in 1740, aged twenty-three, and established a trading business there with his brother, though he is later identified as a sea-captain and customs officer. He was thus neither a full-time architect nor a gentleman amateur. He had learned the rudiments of building from Gibbs, the Hoppus and Cole Palladio, and Langley, and he was paid for the designs he produced. The first evidence of his abilities is the Redwood Library, Newport, of 1749. This is the first American public building based on the Palladian church–temple formula: the portico and flanking half-pediments of its front elevation come from an illustration of a domed garden pavilion by Kent, which was published in his *Designs of Inigo Jones* and appeared again in the

143

143   Peter Harrison: Redwood Library, Newport, Rhode Island, 1749.

Hoppus-Cole. The rear elevation has triple Venetian windows   142
borrowed from Chiswick Villa, which also appeared in Kent's
publication.

The Redwood Library, and Harrison's later buildings – the Gibbs-
inspired King's Chapel, Boston (1749–58), and Brick Market,
Newport (1761), a Jonesian design which was taken from a plate of
Somerset House in *Vitruvius Britannicus* – are characterized by a
bookish eclecticism disengaged from European cultural and ideological concerns. All this was to change with the American Revolution,
which was gathering momentum in 1775, the year of Harrison's
death. For a separate identity was then being moulded for the new
nation, by the great political figure and architect Thomas Jefferson,
who fully appreciated the power of architecture and the potential it
held for society.

Thomas Jefferson (1743–1826) was a highly cultured individual whose flexibility and application of mind make him comparable to the great 'universal men' of the Italian Renaissance. Very little escaped his curiosity, and he had something to say on many important matters, from agriculture and meteorology through to archaeology and philology: he not only reconstructed the first mammoth but made a vast comparative study of Indian dialects. He also applied himself to mechanics and civil engineering. In short, he acquired many of the insights and skills that Vitruvius demanded of an architect. The foundations of classical architecture and a Republican society were to be his most tangible legacies to the future of America.

Jefferson was only fourteen when his father died, leaving him several thousand acres of Virginia farmland and an introduction to politics, having been first citizen in his county. He received a thorough education, which included Greek and Latin, and at the College of William and Mary in Williamsburg he came under the tutelage of an informed group of intellectuals and men of action– Dr William Small, George Wythe and Lieutenant-Governor Fauquier. Wythe introduced Jefferson to the architecture of Richard Taliaferro (pronounced 'Toliver'), his father-in-law, who around 1730 had designed a house in the Wren style at Westover, a variation on the earlier Governor's House in Williamsburg. Taliaferro (1705–79), very much a gentleman-architect, shared a house with Wythe in Williamsburg and was in a position to provide the young Jefferson with some sort of grounding in architecture. There was no manifestation of this for several years, however, until after Jefferson had graduated in law, and was admitted to the bar, in 1767. It was as a newly qualified lawyer that he first turned to architecture in order to build himself a house. His attitude to building reflected the formal education he had received.

His early training in the classics and subsequently in Anglo-Saxon and Roman law were to be recalled frequently in later life, and shaped his view on the potential of American society. As he moved out of law into politics, he increasingly upheld Roman Republicanism as the model around which that society should shape itself. In 1769 he was elected to the Virginia House of Burgesses, and he finally abandoned his law practice in 1774, when he was elected to Virginia's first revolutionary convention.

A split from Britain became inevitable, and Jefferson's politics took on a national significance as he was elected to one of the two Virginia seats at the Second Continental Congress in Philadelphia. There he headed a five-man committee appointed to draft a united 'Declaration of Independence' which, in the form in which it was enacted on 4 July 1776, is taken as a definite reflection of Jefferson's philosophy: of human equality; the natural rights of man; sovereignty of the people; and the right to revolution. In this he was abandoning the dynastic and monarchic élitism of England, and he separated out too the authority of the State from the Church which straight-jacketed European thinking. A new beginning was possible, and antiquity, far from being something in the remote past, was the means to a vigorous future. He succeeded where Gian Giorgio Trissino had failed, and introduced the classical decimal monetary system. Columella-like, he advocated a rectilinear land survey of the States of America in the Land Ordinance. Parallel to the pressing demands of state office, he succeeded in planting the seeds of Roman classicism in America which went beyond the simple empiricism of pattern-book Palladianism.

Before the upheavals of Revolution and Independence, just as he was settling down to practise law, Jefferson began a new house on top of a hill overlooking Charlottesville, on part of the family estate. In his mid-twenties, and with Taliaferro as an example, his ideas revolved around the usual texts: Gibbs's *Rules for Drawing* and *Book of Architecture*, Morris's *Select Architecture*, and the Leoni edition of the *Four Books* were his principal references, and his starting-point was a house plan, after Morris, that was already popular in Virginia.

Surviving drawings of Jefferson's earliest projects show a good understanding of classical ornamentation, and profiles are precisely delineated. The building was to be of brick with timber two-storeyed porticoes, Doric below and Ionic above, at the front and back. In one design the portico form is very close to that of Palladio's Villa Pisani, while another shows service wings enclosing the rear garden in a U shape, in the manner of Villas Zen and Saraceno, though they are set into the hillside and are visible from the garden only as terraces which end with pavilions.

144 68 145

Celebrated houses like Mount Airy and Mount Vernon (which from 1757 onwards took on its present form) had followed the Italian tradition of building villas on high ground. Jefferson made the reference more specific by calling his house 'Monticello'. An eminent French visitor, the Marquis de Chastellux, described the site in 1782:

136

there was nothing . . . to prevent him from fixing his residence wherever he wanted to. But Nature so contrived it, that a Sage and a man of taste should find on his own estate the spot where he might best study and enjoy Her. He called this house *Monticello* (in Italian, Little Mountain), a very modest name indeed, for it is situated on a very high mountain, but a name which bespeaks the owner's attachment to the language of Italy and above all the Fine Arts, of which Italy was the cradle and is still the resort.

Surely it is not coincidental that Palladio had also described the setting
for his Villa Rotonda as 'sopra un monticello' (raised upon a small hill). Could it be that Jefferson had read an Italian edition of the *Quattro libri*, perhaps in a library in Williamsburg, or was he simply translating the idea from his English version of the *Four Books*?

No matter. He had fallen under the spell of Anglo-Palladian architecture, and in Williamsburg, which he visited frequently once he was elected to the House of Burgesses, he made designs for an octagonal chapel, an addition to the College of William and Mary, and revisions to the Governor's residence, guided by Leoni's *Four Books* and Morris's *Select Architecture*.

With the onset of the Revolution the capital was moved inland to Richmond, and in 1776 Jefferson presented a bill to support the design of new buildings for the House of Delegates, composed of three individual structures for the Legislative, Executive and Judiciary. In

144   Jefferson: elevation project for Monticello, before March 1771.

pursuit of this he headed the Building Committee in 1780, and developed a more unified proposal exploring the possibility that the Richmond Capitol should take the form of a temple with end porticoes. As he wrote in his Autobiography, it was his wish that the State should have 'an example of architecture in the classic style of antiquity'. No immediate decision was taken, and after the death of his wife in 1782, after just ten years of marriage, he immersed himself in more wide-ranging national and international issues. In 1784 he was sent as Minister to the Court of France, as a relief to Benjamin Franklin.

He travelled extensively from his base in Paris, to north Italy and England, and while he was impressed with what he saw, he believed that the natural wealth of America offered opportunities that would enable it to surpass Europe, which had suffered centuries of national rivalry and cultural decay since antiquity. Soon after his arrival in Paris, Jefferson published his *Notes on the State of Virginia*, to proclaim the natural advantages of the New World and to refute the accusations of Buffon that America was doomed to degeneracy, and of Corneille de Pauw that the land was so inferior that it could not support a civilization. 'The least vigorous European is more than a match for the strongest American', taunted de Pauw. Instead of prejudiced opinion, Jefferson wished to present 'facts . . . to a candid world'. He submitted that not only was American Nature superior to

145   Jefferson: plan project for the principal floor of Monticello, with two arms of raised terraces and pavilions arranged around a garden court, before August 1772.

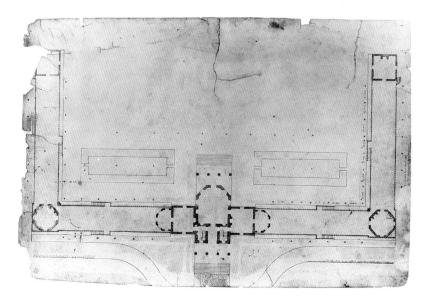

Europe's (he listed the comparative sizes of the bear, bison and elk), but her natural wealth was based on an agricultural economy which would support the new physiocratic society sought after by 18th-century economists who advocated a celebration of the simple life, and government according to natural order, to avoid the evils that afflicted urban society especially in the Old World (high taxation, land and property speculation, imperialism and empires), whilst nourishing and safeguarding individual and collective virtue. To his way of thinking every American could adopt the philosophy of a Fabius, Cato or Pliny and tend his farm for the benefit of the family and individual self-contentment.

Jefferson sought enlightenment in the pristine sanctity of antiquity and Republicanism. There were few positive lessons that contemporary Europe could teach America. He admired France for her buildings, but he complained that architecture in England was 'in the most wretched style I ever saw'. This may explain why he did not feel compelled to see the buildings of Palladio when he was in north Italy, and chose instead to fill his pockets with grains of Italian rice to sow on his return to America. What did nourish him was the remains of antique buildings. When in Nîmes in southern France, he gazed for 'whole hours . . . like a lover at his mistress' at the Roman temple known as the Maison Carrée, which he was to continue to admire through recent drawings of it published by Charles-Louis Clérisseau in his *Antiquités de France, Monuments de Nîmes*, of 1778. Inigo Jones too had spent most of his time in Italy studying ancient Roman buildings: he stayed in Rome for more than six months, but spent only days in Vicenza. Both men were more interested in the principles underlying antique architecture than in modern reworkings of antique precedent.

Whilst Jefferson was in France, the Virginia Legislature amended the bill for the Richmond Capitol in favour of one single structure rather than three. Jefferson was asked to find an appropriate design. He could think of no better model than the Maison Carrée, which, as he wrote to James Madison, is 'one of the most beautiful, if not the most beautiful and precious morsel of architecture left us by antiquity . . . it is very simple, but is noble beyond expression, and would have done honor to any country.' Beauty was no idle thing for Jefferson. By introducing such a great work to America it was his wish 'to improve the taste of my countrymen, to increase their reputation, to reconcile to them the respect of the world, and procure them its praise'.

To this end Jefferson approached Clérisseau and requested that he make a plaster model of the Maison Carrée at a scale of 5 feet to one inch, which, on completion, was sent to Richmond along with plans by Jefferson in 1786. The building was finished in 1796, with a number of changes from the antique original. Clérisseau 'modernized' some details externally, and Jefferson provided an internal layout having three separate 'apartments' for the Legislative, Executive and Judiciary, arranged around a central atrium. Here, where a statue of a Roman god would have been located in the temple, a statue of George Washington was placed, illuminated by a skylight. Windows were located in the side walls to light the interior. The depth of the giant portico was reduced from the four columns of the original to three, and the order was changed from Corinthian to Ionic.

147
148

The depth of the portico may have been reduced for economic reasons. Certainly the justification for the change of order was pragmatic: 'on account of the difficulty of the Corinthian capitals'. Jefferson was unhappy about the final form of the Ionic capitals: 'I yielded, with reluctance, to the taste of Clerissault, in his preference of the modern capital of Scamozzi to the more noble capital of antiquity.' Clérisseau (like Jones and Burlington before him) preferred the version with angled volutes, whereas Jefferson followed the usual practice of Palladio and the ancients in designing volutes parallel to the wall plane, even at the corners, as his drawings for the Ionic order at Monticello and his own early elevations for Richmond confirm.

His veneration for antique ornament did not interfere with his admiration for the advances in house planning in France. He was 'violently smitten' with the Hôtel de Salm by Pierre Rousseau (which, with the Revolution, became the Palais de la Légion d'Honneur), just across the Seine from the Tuileries, which was being finished during the first two years of his stay in Paris. He was struck by its form: a domed room centred on a long rectangular building, with arms extending back to enclose a courtyard. There is no doubt that Jefferson approved of the simplicity of the new generation of houses in France, since he described their positive attributes:

153

All the new and good houses are of a single story that is of the height of 16. [feet] and 18f. generally, and the whole of it is given to rooms of entertainment; but in parts where there are bedrooms they have two tiers of them of 8. to 10f. high each, with a small private staircase. By these means

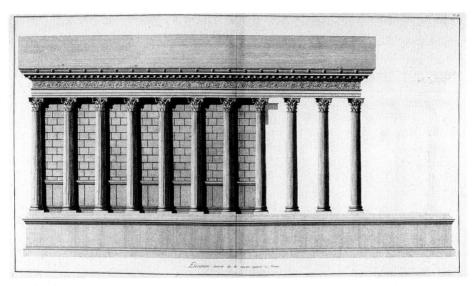

146 Clérisseau: side elevation of the Maison Carrée, Nîmes, from *Antiquités de France*, 1778.
148 *opposite* Jefferson: view of the Virginia Capitol, Richmond, 1786–96. (Wings have since been added.) As built, the Ionic capitals have angled volutes.
147 Jefferson: design for the side elevation of the Virginia Capitol, 1785. There are no pilasters, and the Ionic order has straight volutes. Jefferson frequently used graph paper to ensure accurate right angles and dimensions.

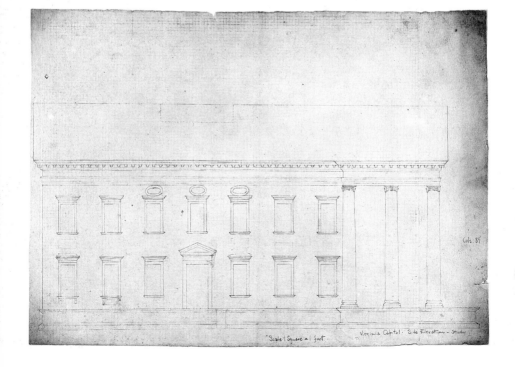

149   Robert Morris: 'A Profile of a Building for a Garden or Summer-House',
from *Select Architecture*, 1755.

great staircases are avoided, which are expensive and occupy a space which
would make a good room in every story.

151   On his return to America he initiated plans to modify Monticello.
144   It is not certain whether the version with two-storeyed porticoes had
already been built; but now his conception for the villa was that it
should have a single storey of accommodation. What he built
150   between 1793 and 1809 seems in fact to have been influenced more by
149   a plate in Morris's *Select Architecture* than by any specific French
example, and the final Monticello bears comparison with suburban
villas around London – like Mount Clare at Roehampton by Sir
Robert Taylor – designed in the 1770s for the new wealthy mercantile
classes.

        Jefferson was not opposed to everything that emanated from
Britain and, indeed, he developed a fascination for early Anglo-Saxon
history and was a positive enthusiast of Whig culture. To Jefferson,
the Anglo-Saxon settlers of England were like the first settlers of
America: they lived free according to their own rules until the
invading Normans imposed on them alien rule and feudalism. He
compared the Anglo-Saxons generically with the Whigs, the
Normans with the Tories. The Tories were 'weakly and nerveless, the

150 Jefferson: west or garden front of Monticello, 1793–1809. The domed octagon contains a single room at high level and has no volumetric impact on the ground floor room beneath.

151 Jefferson: plan project for Monticello, 1796?, showing the house much as it was built.

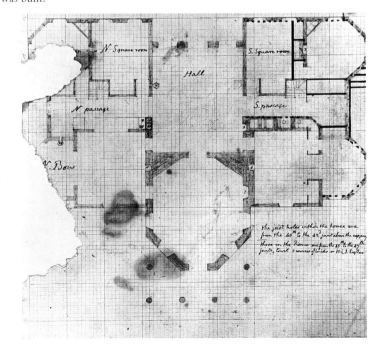

rich and the corrupt seeing more safety and accessibility in a strong executive'; the Whigs, conversely, were 'healthy, firm and virtuous, feeling confidence in their physical and moral resources, and willing to part with only so much power as is necessary for their good government, and therefore to retain the rest in the hands of the many.'

Following the prophets of Enlightenment, like Francis Bacon, Newton, Locke and Shaftesbury, Jefferson's sympathies and encouragement were for the 'whig' in mankind. Indeed, his individualistic approach to antiquity in architecture was directly comparable to the early work of the professed Whig Lord Burlington. Burlington designed Chiswick Villa based on Roman prototypes, and the York Assembly Rooms based on the Vitruvian account of the Egyptian Hall: Jefferson designed Monticello similarly, and adapted an actual antique temple for the Richmond Capitol. But Jefferson, unlike Burlington, had no equivalent of William Kent to develop the interiors of his designs, and he relied heavily on his extensive library, marking plates in the *Edifices antiques de Rome* by Desgodetz, and in Errard and Fréart de Chambray's *Parallèle de l'architecture antique avec la moderne*, so that his interior decorators might have models for friezes and other ornaments in the principal rooms at Monticello. Jefferson probably felt there was no compromise in this procedure, and, in any case, preferred what he perceived as 'Roman simplicity' to the rich, flamboyant interiors which Kent had created.

Other house designs followed. Advising General John Hartwell Cocke who was building a house for himself, Bremo, in 1816, Jefferson clearly promoted Palladianism: Palladio, he declared, was 'the Bible. You should get it and stick close to it.' He went on to show how the 'Bible' might be interpreted in relation to the proposed house:

The rule was that the height of a room should be equal to its width – 20 ft. would not be too much but 16 ft would do – his were 18 ft . . . The Italian rule for windows is a third of the whole space: 7 feet of light to every 21 feet of wall. . . . The Tuscan order was too plain – it would do for your Barns &c but was not fit for a dwelling House. The Doric would not cost much more and would be vastly handsomer. You could get drawings of the columns, cornices &c from him.

This was, of course, Palladianism made simple for a less erudite enthusiast than himself. Jefferson's own design principles were more sophisticated: his architecture was intended to reflect natural order and to be employed for the betterment of society.

Whilst his preference was for small agrarian-based communities, he made plans for extending the city of Richmond in 1780, in an ordered, systematic way which takes on the formal characteristics of Roman city planning. Spaces within the city, he proposed, should be alternately occupied by landscape or building lots, taking 'the chequerboard for a plan. Let the black squares only be building squares, and the white ones be left open, in turf and trees. Every square of houses will front an open square. . . . The plan of the town . . . will be found handsome and pleasant.'

Nine years later, on returning from his diplomatic mission to France, as Secretary of State he proposed a general development plan for Washington, the nation's new capital on the Potomac, as well as sites for the President's House and the Capitol, the offices and public walks. His own preference was for rectangular building lots, 50 × 71 feet (71 feet being the diagonal of a 50-foot square), with a controlled maximum height for buildings. But designing Washington fell to the French émigré Pierre Charles L'Enfant (1754–1825), and Jefferson was empowered to do little more than make available to L'Enfant the plans he had collected together of the major European cities.

When he was elected President in 1801 he made direct and immediate improvements to Pennsylvania Avenue, planting rows of trees along it in the manner of the Parisian boulevards. L'Enfant had by then been dismissed, and Jefferson appointed an English-trained architect, Benjamin Henry Latrobe (1764–1820), as Surveyor of Public Buildings. They worked jointly on the Capitol building between 1803 and 1809 making changes to the original design. This relationship cannot always have been easy, as Latrobe had been trained in the Neoclassical style that had superseded Palladianism as the dominant architecture of England, and drew on a more broadly based classicism than the Roman antiquity that Jefferson and other Palladians had referred to.

When the design of the Capitol was still under L'Enfant's control, Jefferson had written encouraging him to follow an antique model which had 'the approbation of thousands of years'. For the President's House, on the other hand, he preferred 'the celebrated fronts of modern buildings, which have already received the approbation of all good judges. Such as the Galerie du Louvre, the Garde Meubles, and the two fronts of the Hôtel de Salm.' Yet when a design competition 153 was held for the President's House he himself submitted, quite anonymously, a design highly dependent on the version of the Villa 154

199

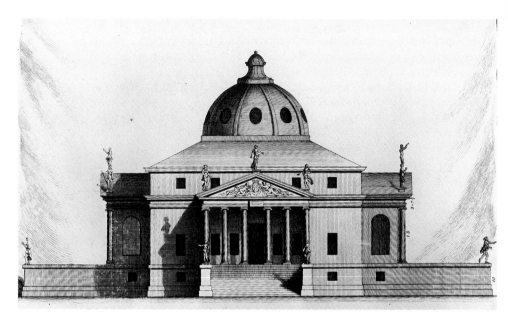

152   Leoni: the Villa Rotonda, from *The Architecture of Andrea Palladio*, 1716–20.

154   *opposite* Jefferson: competition design for the President's House, Washington, 1792. A cumbersome reinterpretation of the Villa Rotonda after Leoni. The plan is stretched, the dome and lantern heightened, and the reorganization of the fenestration expedient rather than delightful.

153   Pierre Rousseau: river front of the Hôtel de Salm, Paris, 1782–86.

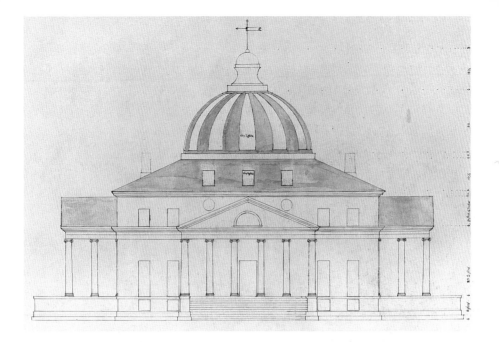

Rotonda in Leoni's *Four Books* – an Anglo-Italian proposition far 152
removed from any of his own recommendations.

A few years later he returned to the idea of a centralized house for
his retreat at Poplar Forest, near Lynchburg. Unlike his rejected 156,157
design for the President's House, this was as inspired and precise as any
of the centralized Palladian villa forms. His plan of 1806 is octagonal,
having a '50 f. diameter', which at its centre has a 20 × 20 × 20-foot
cubic dining room. This room is placed at the entry level and is top-lit
because it is surrounded by bedrooms and a drawing-room. A
basement beneath takes advantage of the slope on which the house is
placed, and is provided with natural light and ventilation. The most
likely source is a design for an octagonal house which appeared in
William Kent's *Designs of Inigo Jones*. However, Jefferson's control of 155
the overall symmetry is superior, and unlike many of its centralized
predecessors Poplar Forest was intended to be eminently habitable. As
Jefferson wrote of it in 1812, 'When finished, it will be the best
dwellinghouse in the state, except that of Monticello; perhaps
preferable to that, as more proportioned to the faculties of a private
citizen.'

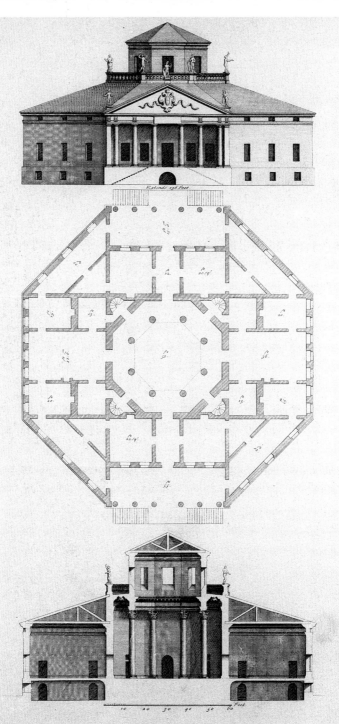

Extends 136 Feet

10 20 30 40 50 60 Feet

I. Iones Architectus   H. Flitcroft Delin.   H. Hulsbergh Sculp.

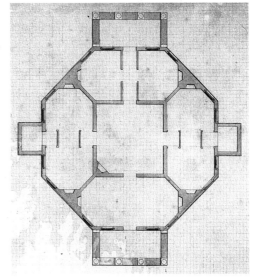

156, 157 Jefferson: garden elevation and sketch plan of Poplar Forest, Virginia, begun 1806. The plan, of the principal floor, was drawn *c.* 1820 by Jefferson's daughter, Cornelia Jefferson Randolph.

155 *opposite* Inigo Jones: design for an octagonal house, from Kent's *The Designs of Inigo Jones*, 1727.

A concern for the 'private citizen' was behind every move Jefferson made, architectural and political. He wanted a nation of self-government to reflect individual choice and the needs of society. This is the only route to contentment: 'happiness is the aim of life, and virtue is the foundation of happiness', he wrote. This humanism and regard for classical *virtù* culminated in his foundation of the University of Virginia.

He had believed in the need for an educated society for some time, and had introduced a 'Bill for the more General Diffusion of Knowledge' into the Virginia legislature back in 1779. As he wrote to John Adams in 1813, the new society should not have an 'artificial' aristocracy 'founded on wealth and birth' but a 'natural' aristocracy based on 'virtue and talents'. His intentions paralleled the academies initiated in Renaissance Italy, where centres of excellence grew up under the patronage of a Medici or a Trissino. Yet Jefferson had in mind something more wide-reaching and on the scale of a university.

His thoughts on the ideal university where virtue and talents may be fostered were clear by the first term of his presidency. Early in 1805, he envisaged an 'academical village' where students could develop a close relationship with their professors. Here, contrary to the monastery-like colleges of Oxford and Cambridge, there would be no representation of the Church: the university 'will be based on the illimitable freedom of the human mind . . . for here we are not afraid to follow the truth wherever it may lead or to tolerate any error so long as reason is left free to combat it.' Progress was made towards this end on some two hundred acres of land west of Charlottesville, which was within sight of Monticello. It was a location of which Vitruvius would have approved: 'high, dry, open, furnished with good water, and nothing in its vicinity which would threaten the health of the students'. The foundation stone of the University of Virginia was laid on 6 October 1817, with Jefferson and two former presidents, James Madison and James Monroe, present.

The master-plan Jefferson drew reflects the 'academical village' notion:

We propose to lay off a square or rather 3 sides of a square about 7— or 800 f. wide, leaving it open at one end to be extended indefinitely. On the closed end, and on the two sides we propose to arrange separate pavilions for each professor and his school. Each pavilion is to have a schoolroom below, and 2 rooms for the professor above; and between pavilion and pavilion a range of dormitories for the students, one story high giving to each a room 10 f. wide and 14 f. deep, the pavilions about 36 f. wide in front, and 24 f. in depth.

The steep site did not allow a true square to be formed, and a long, narrow open space was formed instead, 200 feet wide and 600 feet long on the north–south axis following the slope of the hill. This gently terraced, grassed space – called the 'Lawn' – is open to the south (or was, until 1901) and closed to the north by a Pantheon-like building, the Rotunda; along its length it is lined by two colonnades which provide a covered passage in front of the dormitories, alternating with the porticoes of five two-storeyed pavilions. Jefferson wanted the ten pavilions to be 'models of taste and good architecture' and of different compositions 'so as to serve as specimens for the Architectural lecturer'. He invited suggestions from an eminent Washington architect, Dr William Thornton (1759–1828), and from Latrobe, and incorporated their ideas for six of the pavilions. The ornamentation was heavily reliant once again on the plates in Leoni's edition of Palladio's *Four Books*, and Errard and Fréart de Chambray's *Parallèle*. The orders of the five West Lawn Pavilions – I, III, V, VII and IX – are the Doric of the Baths of Diocletian (Fréart), Corinthian (Palladio), Ionic (Palladio), Doric (Palladio),

160

161,163

158,159

158   Jefferson: detail of Pavilion I of the University of Virginia, finished 1822.

159   Fréart de Chambray: the Doric order of the Baths of Diocletian, from the *Parallèle*, 1650.

and Ionic of the Temple of Fortuna Virilis (Palladio). Those of the East Lawn – II, IV, VI, VIII and X – are the Ionic of the Temple of Fortuna Virilis (Palladio) again, and the Doric of Albano, Ionic of the Theatre of Marcellus, Corinthian of the Baths of Diocletian, and Doric of the Theatre of Marcellus (all from Fréart). Latrobe provided designs for Pavilions III, V, VIII, IX and X; Thornton for Pavilion VII. (The numbers start at the closed north end.)

Jefferson's architectural concept may have been influenced by the twelve pavilions (one for each calendar month) surrounding a lawn at Louis XIV's château at Marly; and if so, his decision to build ten pavilions may have been a 'rational' decimalization of that device. He introduced another 'improvement', as can be seen from the Peter Maverick plan made before 1822: the number of rooms which make up the dormitories increases towards the open end, from four to six to seven to eight and ten (the final dormitory has eight rooms on the east side and ten on the west). From the closed end, the pavilions consequently appear to be evenly spaced, an effect which may be compared to the 'streets in perspective' constructed by Scamozzi for Palladio's Teatro Olimpico in Vicenza. The 'science' and 'virtues' celebrated at the Teatro Olimpico are realized by Jefferson in a new form dedicated to knowledge and wisdom, which opens out towards the Virginia landscape at one end, and focuses on a microcosm of Nature – the Rotunda – at the other.

160

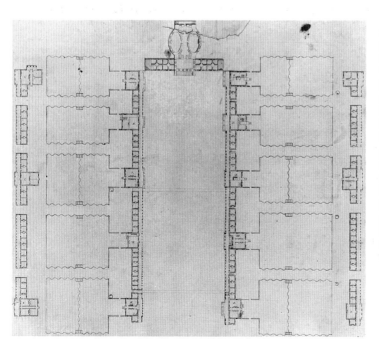

160 Jefferson: plan of the University of Virginia, Charlottesville (drawing for the Maverick plan, before 1822). The Rotunda and pavilions linked by colonnades frame the terraced Lawn. Behind the pavilions are gardens enclosed by brick serpentine or 'crinkle-crankle' walls.

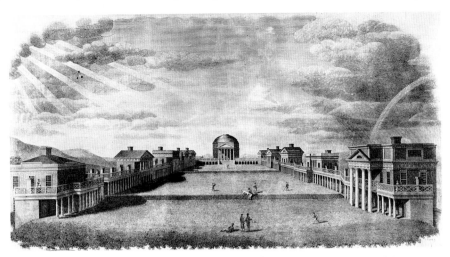

161 Jefferson: the University of Virginia. Engraving by B. Tanner, 1827.

The Rotunda was begun six years into the building programme, in 1823. The idea that there should be a focus to the Lawn had come from Latrobe, though it was Jefferson who determined that in contrast to the 'cubic' pavilions this should be an exemplar of 'spherical' architecture. Jefferson considered the Maison Carrée a principal example of the 'cubic' in architecture, while for the 'spherical' there could be no finer precedent than the Pantheon in Rome. Jefferson turned to his Leoni for guidance, and ordered a copy of the more recent study of the Pantheon by Giovanni Battista Piranesi, which was to arrive too late to be instrumental in the final design.

The Pantheon was a much larger building than was required at Charlottesville, so the Rotunda was made half the size of the original. The Pantheon was experienced as an interior space embedded in a dense urban fabric, whereas the Rotunda was subdivided by floors and rooms internally, and was prominently displayed on a height. (The interior was altered after a fire in 1895, but restored to Jefferson's original scheme in 1973.) The implied sphere of the Pantheon's interior was consequently applied by Jefferson to the exterior of the Rotunda, where it can be fully appreciated: his building is explicitly 'round', as the Richmond Capitol and University pavilions express outwardly their 'cubic' qualities. Internally, the lower two floors contained a gymnasium and lecture rooms; it was only in the library room on the upper level that the rotundity manifested itself, and

163

40
162

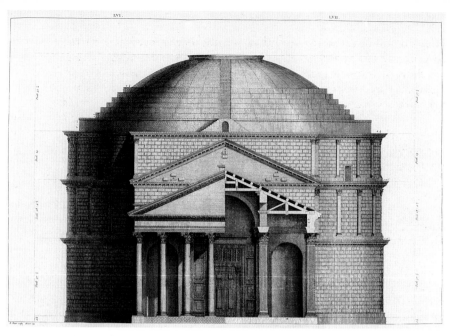

162 Leoni: the Pantheon, Rome, from *The Architecture of Andrea Palladio*, 1716–20.

163 Jefferson: elevation project for the Rotunda, University of Virginia, 1819.

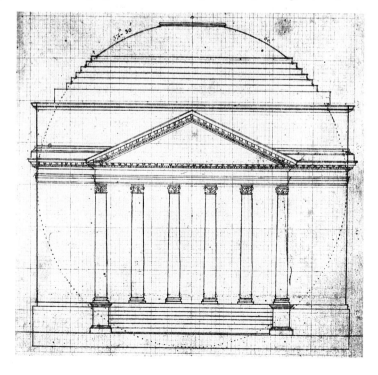

Jefferson imbued the space with a significance appropriate to the programme. The domed ceiling was to have been painted sky-blue as a backdrop to gilt planets and stars moved by a mechanical system under the direction of an operator. This planetarium was supported on paired pillars, behind which were stacked the University's collection of books. The central oculus might be taken to represent the sun. Just as the sun is the fount of Nature and the centre of the 'mechanical' universe, so the library itself is the source of enlightenment and wisdom. In a university without the presence of the Church, the Rotunda is representative of the elemental authority of Nature and the power of Reason.

Jefferson was concerned with representing the purity of Nature and natural form in his architecture, and doing so as explicitly as possible, which took him towards the 'elementalism' – the quest for pure geometry – of 18th-century French theory. The spirit of antiquity is always manifest in his designs, however, as it was in the architecture of his more principled Palladian predecessors. Ultimately, this essential spirit transcends form. As the first Rector wrote in 1820, in defence of the emblem that had been chosen for the University:

The engraving in the field is a Minerva, inventress and protectress of the arts, enrobed in her Peplum, with an olive branch in one hand and a cornucopia in the other, emblems of peace, plenty & wisdom. Our living sister Wm. & Mary [College at Williamsburg] complains that we had pilfered her device; her seal being the temple of Minerva. We say NO. She chose the temple, we the Goddess; she the shell, we the kernel. The votaries of the temple will go there, those of the goddess here.

Although Jefferson possibly never knew the Barbaro Tempietto at Maser, or the centralized projects by Palladio for the Redentore in Venice, on which it was based, both architects achieved in their final buildings a tangible testament to Vitruvian classical principles. Moreover, the humanism that Jefferson displayed in his politics and architecture truly affected society in a way that the first age of humanism could only aspire to do. The architecture of English Palladianism tended to reinforce the political mores of the time. But Jefferson, the last exponent, and himself a thorough embodiment of classical *virtù*, achieved the Declaration of Independence, religious liberty in Virginia, and the founding and building of the University of Virginia. These were the three accomplishments by which he wished to be remembered, and they are a fitting epitaph, too, to the Vitruvio-Palladianism of the English-speaking world.

Parts One to Three: Palladio

Primary sources

ALBERTI, Leon Battista, *I dieci libri dell'architettura*, transl. Pietro Lauro, Venice, 1546
—*L'architettura (De re aedificatoria) di Leon Battista Alberti*, transl. Cosimo Bartoli, Florence, 1550
—*On the art of building in ten books*, transl. J. Rykwert, N. Leach and R. Tavernor, Cambridge, Mass., 1988
—*On painting and On sculpture*, ed. and transl. C. Grayson, London, 1972
AUGUSTINE, St, *The city of God*, transl. H. Bettenson, Harmondsworth, 1972
BERTOTTI-SCAMOZZI, Ottavio, *Le fabbriche e i disegni di Andrea Palladio...*, Vicenza, 1776–83 (facsimile of 1796 ed., London, 1968)
GUALDO, Paolo, 'Vita di Andrea Palladio', ed. Giovanni Montenari, in Montenari, *Del Teatro Olimpico di Andrea Palladio in Vicenza*, 2nd ed., Padua, 1749
PALLADIO, Andrea, *I quattro libri dell'architettura*, Venice, 1570 (facsimile ed., Milan, 1980)
—*Scritti minori*, ed. L. Puppi, Milan, 1989
SCAMOZZI, Vincenzo, *L'idea della architettura universale*, Venice, 1615
SERLIO, Sebastiano, *Tutte l'opere d'architettura et prospettiva*, Venice, 1584, another ed. 1619
TRISSINO, Gian Giorgio, *L'Italia liberata dai Gotthi*, Rome and Venice 1547, 1548
VASARI, Giorgio, *Le vite de' più eccellenti pittori, scultori e architettori* (rev. ed.), Florence, 1568. English ed. *Lives of the artists*, transl. George Bull, Harmondsworth, 1987
VITRUVIUS, *De Lucio Vitruvio Pollione de architectura libri dece*, transl. with a commentary by Cesare Cesariano, Como, 1521
—*I dieci libri dell'architettura*, transl. with commentary by Daniele Barbaro, Venice, 1556

Secondary sources

ACKERMAN, James S., *Palladio*, Harmondsworth and Baltimore, 1966
Alvise Cornaro ed il suo tempo, exh. cat., Padua, 1980
BAXANDALL, Michael, *Painting and experience in fifteenth-century Italy*, Oxford, 1980
BURNS, Howard, et al., *Andrea Palladio, 1508–1580: the portico and the farmyard*, exh. cat., London, Arts Council of Great Britain, 1975
CAMPBELL, Ian, 'St Peter's, Rome', *Oxford Art Journal*, 1981, pp. 3–8
CARPEGGIANI, P., ed., *Alvise Cornaro, scritti sull'architettura*, Padua, 1980
CONSTANT, Caroline, *The Palladio Guide*, Princeton, 1985/London 1988
FOSCARI, A. and Tafuri, M., *L'armonia e i conflitti*, Turin, 1983
HOLBERTON, Paul, *Palladio's villas: life in the Renaissance countryside*, London, 1990
HOWARD, Deborah. 'Four centuries of literature on Palladio', *Journal of the Soc. of Architectural Historians*, 39, 1980, pp. 224–41
—*Jacopo Sansovino; architecture and patronage in Renaissance Venice*, New Haven, 1975
—*The architectural history of Venice*, London, 1980
—and Longair, M., 'Harmonic proportion and Palladio's *Quattro libri*', *Journal of the Soc. of Architectural Historians*, 41, 1982, pp. 116–43
KRAUTHEIMER, Richard, 'Alberti's Templum Etruscum', *Studies in Early Christian, Medieval and Renaissance Art*, New York and London, 1969, pp. 65–72
LEWIS, Carolyn Kolb, *Villa Giustinian at Roncade*, New York and London, 1977
LEWIS, Douglas, *The drawings of Andrea Palladio*, International Exhibitions Foundation, 1981
MARTINI, A., *Manuale di metrologia ossia misure, pesi e monete in uso attualmente e anticamente*, Turin, 1883 (repr. Rome, 1976)
McANDREW, John, *Venetian architecture of the Early Renaissance*, Cambridge, Mass., 1980
MORSOLIN, B., *Gian Giorgio Trissino. Monografia di un gentiluomo letterato nel secolo XVI*, Florence, 1894
PUPPI, Lionello, *Andrea Palladio*, Milan, 1973
ROSENTHAL, E. 'The house of Andrea Mantegna in Mantua', *Gazette des Beaux-Arts*, LX, 1962, pp. 327–48
RYKWERT, Joseph, 'Andrea Palladio: the three Venetian churches', *Domus*, 609, Sept., 1980, pp. 28–31
—and Tavernor, R., 'Sant' Andrea at Mantua', *Architects' Journal*, no.21, vol. 183, 21 May 1986, pp. 36–57

SINDING-LARSEN, S., 'Palladio's Redentore: a compromise in composition', *Art Bulletin*, 1965, pp. 419–37

—'Some functional and iconographical aspects of the centralised church in the Italian Renaissance', *Acta ad archaeologiam et artium historium pertinentia, Institutum Romanum Norvegiae*, II, 1965, pp. 203 ff.

Splendours of the Gonzagas, exh. cat., ed. D. Chambers and J. Martineau, London, Victoria and Albert Museum, 1982

TAFURI, Manfredo, *Venezia e il Rinascimento: religione, scienza, architettura*, Turin, 1985

WIEBENSON, Dora, ed., *Architectural theory and practice from Alberti to Ledoux*, Chicago, 1982

WITTKOWER, Rudolf, *Architectural principles in the Age of Humanism*, London, 1977

ZORZI, Gian Giorgio, *I disegni delle antichità di Andrea Palladio*, Venice, 1959

—*Le opere pubbliche e i palazzi privati di Andrea Palladio*, Venice, 1965

—*Le chiese e i ponti di Andrea Palladio*, Venice, 1967

—*Le ville e i teatri di Andrea Palladio*, Venice, 1969

Parts Four to Six: Palladianism

Primary sources

BURLINGTON, Earl of, *Fabbriche antiche disegnate da Andrea Palladio Vicentine*, London, 1730

CAMPBELL, Colen, *Vitruvius Britannicus*, London, 1715–25

—*First book of Palladio*, London, 1728

—*Andrea Palladio's Five orders of architecture*, 1729 [1728]

CLÉRISSEAU, C. L., *Antiquités de France, monuments de Nîmes*, 1778

DESGODETZ, A. B., *Les édifices antiques de Rome*, Paris, 1682 (Jefferson used the London, 1771–95 ed.)

FRÉART DE CHAMBRAY, Roland, and Errard, Charles, *Parallèle de l'architecture antique et de la moderne*, Paris, 1650 (Jefferson used the Paris, 1764–66 ed.)

GIBBS, James, *A book of architecture containing designs of buildings and ornaments*, London, 1728

—*Rules for drawing the several parts of architecture*, London, 1732

HALFPENNY, William, *Practical architecture*, London [*c.*1720]

HOPPUS, Edward, and Cole, Benjamin, *Andrea Palladio's architecture in four books, carefully revis'd and redelineated*, London, 1733–35

JEFFERSON, Thomas, *Notes on the state of Virginia*, Paris, 1782 [1784], London, 1787

JONES, Inigo, annotated copies:
PALLADIO, *L'antichità di roma di M. Andrea Palladio*, Venice, 1588 (Worcester College, Oxford)

—*I quattro libri dell'architettura*, Venice, 1601 (Worcester College, Oxford)

SCAMOZZI, *L'idea della architettura universale*, Venice, 1615 (Worcester College, Oxford)

SERLIO, *Tutte l'opere d'architettura et prospettiva*, Venice, 1600 (Canadian Center for Architecture, Montreal)

VIOLA ZANINI, *Della architettura*, Padua, 1629 (Worcester College, Oxford)

KENT, William, *The designs of Inigo Jones, with some additional designs*, London, 1727

LANGLEY, Batty, *Ancient architecture, restored and improved*, London, 1741 (republ. as *Gothic Architecture*, 1747)

LEONI, Giacomo, *The architecture of Andrea Palladio in four books, . . . to which are added several notes . . . by Inigo Jones*, London, 1715[16]–20

LOCKE, John, *An essay concerning human understanding*, London, 1690

MORRIS, Robert, *An essay in defence of ancient architecture*, London, 1728

—*Lectures on architecture. Consisting of rules founded upon harmonick and arithmetical proportions in building*, London, 1734/36

—*Rural architecture*, 1750 (republ. as *Select Architecture*, 1755 and 1757)

—*The architectural remembrancer*, London, 1751

POPE, Alexander, *Epistle to Burlington*, London, 1731

SHAFTESBURY, 3rd Earl of, 'Soliloquy: or, advice to an author', in *The life, unpublished letters and philosophical regimen of Anthony, Earl of Shaftesbury*, ed. B. Rand, London, 1900

SHUTE, John, *The first and chief groundes of architecture*, London, 1563

VILLALPANDO, J. B., *De postrema Ezechialis prophetae visione*, Rome, 1605

VIOLA ZANINI, Giuseppe, *Della architettura*, Padua, 1629

WARE, Isaac, *The four books of Andrea Palladio's architecture*, London, 1738

—*Designs of Inigo Jones and others*, London [*c.* 1731]

WEBB, John, *The most notable antiquity of Great Britain, vulgarly called Stone-Heng on Salisbury Plain, restored by Inigo Jones Esq.*, London, 1655

—*A vindication of Stone-Heng restored*, London, 1665

WREN, Christopher, *Parentalia: or memoirs of the family of the Wrens*, London, 1750

WOTTON, Henry, *The elements of architecture*, London, 1624

Secondary sources

ALLSOPP, B., ed., *Inigo Jones on Palladio*, Newcastle-upon-Tyne, 1970

BOLD, John, *John Webb*, Oxford, 1989

CERUTTI-FUSCO, Annarosa, *Inigo Jones Vitruvius Britannicus*, Rimini, 1985

COLVIN, Howard, *A biographical dictionary of British architects, 1600–1840*, London, 1978

DOWNES, Kerry, *The architecture of Wren*, London, 1982

—'Chiswick Villa', *Architectural Review*, vol. 164, 980, Oct. 1978, pp. 225–36

EISENTHAL, E., 'John Webb's reconstruction of the ancient house', *Architectural History*, 28, 1985, pp. 7–18

FORSSMAN, Erik, 'Il Palladianesimo: un tentativo di definizione', in *Palladio: la sua eredità nel mondo*, Milan, 1980

GIROUARD, Mark, *Robert Smythson and the Elizabethan country house*, New Haven, 1983

HILL, Christopher, *The century of revolution 1603–1714*, Edinburgh, 1960

HARRIS, John, *The Palladians*, London, 1981

—*The design of the English country house, 1620–1920*, London, 1985

—and Higgott, G., *Inigo Jones: complete architectural drawings*, London, 1989

—Orgel, S., and Strong, R., *The King's Arcadia: Inigo Jones and the Stuart Court*, exh. cat., Arts Council of Great Britain, 1973

KIMBALL, S. Fiske, *Thomas Jefferson, architect*, Boston, 1916

LEES-MILNE, J., *Earls of creation*, London, 1962/New York, 1963

MALONE, Dumas, *Jefferson and his time: the sage of Monticello*, Boston, 1977

NICHOLS, Frederick, *Thomas Jefferson's architectural drawings*, Charlottesville, Va., 1984

Palladio: la sua eredità nel mondo, Milan, 1980

PALME, Per, *Triumph of peace: a study of the Banqueting House*, Stockholm, 1956

PÉREZ-GÓMEZ, Alberto, *Architecture and the crisis of modern science*, Cambridge, Mass., 1983

PFISTER, Harold F., 'Burlingtonian architectural theory in England and America', *Winterthur Portfolio II*, Charlottesville, Va., 1976

PIERSON, William H., *American buildings and their architects*, I, New York, 1968

RYKWERT, Joseph, *The first moderns: the architects of the eighteenth century*, Cambridge, Mass., 1980

SCHMIDT, Leo, 'Holkham Hall, Norfolk', *Country Life*, vol. 167, 1980, pp. 214–17 and 298–301

STRONG, Roy, *Britannia triumphans*, London, 1980

STUTCHBURY, Howard, *The architecture of Colen Campbell*, Manchester, 1967

SUMMERSON, John, *Architecture in Britain, 1530–1830*, Harmondsworth, 1970

—*Inigo Jones*, Harmondsworth, 1966

VALMARANA, Mario, 'Il Palladianesimo negli Stati Uniti d'America', in *Palladio: la sua eredità nel mondo*, Milan, 1980

WHITEHILL, Walter M., *Palladio in America*, New York, 1978

WILLIAMS, A. F. B., *The Whig supremacy, 1714–1760*, Oxford, 1962

WILSON JONES, Mark, 'The Tempietto and the roots of coincidence', *Architectural History*, 33, 1990, pp. 1–28

WITTKOWER, Rudolf, *Palladio and English Palladianism*, London and New York, 1974

YEOMANS, D., 'Inigo Jones's roof structures', *Architectural History*, 29, 1986, pp. 85–100

ACKNOWLEDGMENTS FOR ILLUSTRATIONS

Alinari 47

Rijksmuseum, Amsterdam 26

Photo copyright © Wayne Andrews/Esto 136

Maryland Historical Society, Baltimore 154

B. T. Batsford, Ltd 129

Osvaldo Böhm 8

Coolidge Collection, Massachusetts Historical Society, Boston 144, 145, 147, 151

Howard Burns 6, 52

The Master and Fellows, Magdalene College, Cambridge 95

Thomas Jefferson Papers, Special Collections Department, Manuscripts Division, University of Virginia Library, Charlottesville 157, 161, 163

Devonshire Collection, Chatsworth. Reproduced by permission of the Chatsworth Settlement Trustees 73, 83, 86, 87, 96, 97, 102

Edward Diestelkamp 27

Drayton Hall, Charleston, S. C./National Trust for Historic Preservation 141

Gabinetto dei Disegni, Uffizi, Florence 42

INDEX

216